COLUMBUS
F.B.I.
OPERATIVE

**A TRUE STORY
BY T. ARAUJO**

TRAFFORD

National Library of Canada Cataloguing in Publication Data

A cataloguing record for this book that includes the U.S. Library of
Congress Classification number, the Library of Congress Call number
and the Dewey Decimal cataloguing code is available from the National
Library of Canada. The complete cataloguing record can be obtained
from the National Library's online database at: www.nlc-bnc.ca/
amicus/index-e.html

ISBN 1-4120- 2585-0

**This book was published *on-demand* in cooperation with Trafford
Publishing.**
On-demand publishing is a unique process and service of making a book
available for retail sale to the public taking advantage of on-demand
manufacturing and Internet marketing. **On-demand publishing** includes
promotions, retail sales, manufacturing, order fulfilment, accounting and
collecting royalties on behalf of the author.

Suite 6E, 2333 Government St., Victoria, B.C. V8T 4P4, CANADA
Phone   250-383-6864   Toll-free 1-888-232-4444 (Canada & US)
Fax   250-383-6804   E-mail   sales@trafford.com
Web site www.trafford.com   TRAFFORD PUBLISHING IS A DIVISION OF TRAFFORD
                             HOLDINGS LTD.
Trafford Catalogue #04-0413   www.trafford.com/robots/04-0413.html

10   9   8   7   6   5   4   3   2

TABLE OF CONTENTS

INTRODUCTION
TAGGING AND GANGS

"TAGGING" WAS AN historical beginning for contemporary street gangs. "Tagging" began in the summer of 1970 in Manhattan, New York. A youth that went by the name of "Taki 183" began to paint graffiti on a variety of public and private properties. Ice cream trucks and buildings were signature targets for Taki's tag. He had a variety of artistic designs which he would use to mark his targets with first using water resistant markers, and then later replacing the markers with spray paint. On one occasion Taki was interviewed by a New York Times reporter and the Times decided to publish the interview which, in essence, gave rise to Taki's fame. "Other youths became impressed with the notoriety "Taki 183" had received and soon it became a competition for fame" (LAPD 1994).

As the problem with tagging increased, taggers became more creative and distinct with their art and their work began to stand out more. They each developed their own signature way of tagging in order be recognized. Tagging became a more common topic through media, films, videos and books. As youths began to hear and read more about tagging it eventually spread throughout the United States and deeply entrenched itself into inner cities of Los Angeles County.

Taggers are made up predominately of males and a few females known as queens. Reasons for these destructive manners are theoretical but are said to be one of the following: The males are drawn to tagging crews because they seek an extension of family and a desire to "fuel their negative self

esteem". Their young ages allow them to be easily impression-
able and pulled into tagging crews. Their ages will vary but
are usually between thirteen to seventeen years old. Some may
look upon tagging as harmless or victimless. In reality, graffiti
costs taxpayers millions of dollars annually and independent
property owners have had to pay out of their own pockets. "In
the 1990's the Southern Rapid Transit district spent in excess
of nine and a half million dollars annually to battle the tagging
epidemic" (source pg). As the judicial system and law enforcement teamed up to battle and bring tagging under control a
more severe epidemic emerged at an alarming rate. "It wasn't
long before Youth Street Gangs were the most talked about
problem within our society" (FCSO, 1995).

A misconception is that Youth Street Gangs originated in
the late fifties and sixties to become the out-of-control disease
that it is today. Youth Street Gangs actually had its beginnings
during the vast immigration from Europe into the eastern coast
of the UnitedStates in 1910. The west coast was most affected
from 1910 through 1925 when many immigrated from Mexico
to Southern California. Due to economic influence, the Mexican Revolution, and the Great Depression, San Diego and Los
Angeles became heavily populated with Hispanics. The new
immigrants began to settle into areas which were already
populated by other Hispanics with well rooted ties. Rivalries
developed between them and the youth began to divide into
small groups for protection from one another. Competition for
neighborhoods and women fueled insults and adversarial roles.
"Violence between the groups escalated and vendettas became
a more common occurrence" (LASO, 1995).

During the 1930s and 1940s immigration of Hispanics
continued at alarming rates. At this time Los Angeles was
considered to be a military town. Many of the Hispanic males
were forced to compete with the military for the attention of
the young ladies. Rivalries between the "Pachucos" (young
Hispanic males) and members of the military began to escalate
(LASO, 1996). The most infamous incident was the murders
of "Sleepy Lagoon" of 1940. Formerly known as "Sleepy

Lagoon", it was William's Ranch of Montebello, California where violence erupted between members of the military and the 38th Street Gang AKA, the "Zoot Suiters". Competition for the ladies between the military and the "Zoot Suiters" became more intense and heated. Violence erupted at an all time high resulting in a riot. Young Hispanic males were in a two step disadvantage. First, the military wore uniforms that were attractive to the young ladies. This influenced the young Hispanic males to create their very own stylized dress called the "Zoot Suit". Secondly, the members of the military had regular income to spend with the young ladies. The young Hispanics were forced to become creative in earning or hustling money in order to compete. After the event of "Sleepy Lagoon", the gangs began to better organize. They developed a signature dress and created their own coded language known as calo, a combination of English and Spanish. The gangs became more sophisticated and enterprising. They became involved with illegal activities and deeply entrenched themselves with illicit drug trade. The drug trade created the large volume of cash flow which they needed to finance their appetite for luxury items, clothes, women and power. This situation created a desperate need for society to find more innovative ways of dealing with the effects of the illegal drug trade; this lead to the United States Department of Justice forming the Drug Enforcement Administration in 1973. Their mission was to exclusively investigate drug related offenses.

PROLOGUE

As a child growing up in the great whaling city of New Bedford, Massachusetts I came into contact with the negative effects of illegal drugs, its horror, and destruction. My cousin Maria Furtado had emigrated here from Sao Miguel, Azores, Portugal during the 1960s as had much of my family. She was very pretty with long brown hair, average weight and height with a sparkling smile, and full of life. She, as do all immigrants that come to the United States, had a potentially promising future to look forward to.

It didn't take her long to get wrapped up into the drug culture. It was easy and inviting for her because two of her brothers who arrived here a few years before were already deeply involved in dealing drugs. She eventually became addicted to drugs, and was introduced to prostitution. Her lifestyle led to an arrest and conviction that she served out in a prison near Boston. She pled out her charges as most defendants do in order to receive a lesser sentence. Part of her plea agreement was to disclose who her narcotics contacts were. Upon her release from prison she was found dead the next morning in a Boston motel room, a punishment for informing. As of this day her assailant has not been brought to trial. Although she and I didn't have a close relationship I still cared for her; after all she was family. Her unjustified and untimely death would be the first block among many that would compile in a foundation of my hate for street drugs.

For the second time in my early life the effects of dangerous and illicit street drugs would affect me even though I had traveled half way around the world. While I was fulfilling my enlistment in the U.S. Army I was stationed in Okinawa with the First Special Forces Group. One evening as I was coming back from a movie with a couple of friends, we arrived at the barracks to find an ambulance loading up one of our buddies Joe. The next morning we received word that he had died of arsenic poisoning. We were dumbfounded to learn Joe had been shooting Heroin into his veins. There were never any signs to indicate that he was an addict. Apparently his addiction was closely guarded.

Over the years Heroin in its pure form had been diluted with various other chemicals in order to make it more profitable for the dealers and more marketable for the users on the streets. During the early 1970s the drug culture went through a phase of diluting the Heroin with Arsenic. If too much Arsenic was used in the cutting process it would cause poisoning resulting in death as with what happened to Joe. His military occupation was repairing and packing parachutes. Soldiers who do this type of work are known as Riggers. The Riggers in our unit were very tightly knit and for some reason they were most affected by what is known as a drug culture hit. In the eighteen months I served with the 1st SFG they lost two more Riggers to drugs and one whose overdose almost killed him.

On October ninth, nineteen hundred and seventy-three, I left Okinawa for an assignment at Fort Bragg, North Carolina. It wasn't long before I realized there was a drug problem there as well. I voluntarily left Special Forces and volunteered to work in an undercover capacity for the Third Region Criminal Investigations Command, Fort Bragg Field Office. My undercover assignment was with Corps Support Command, S-3 Training as a clerk. My orders were to gather information on drug dealings on the base and anyone dealing to military personnel. After spending five and a half months of working several small drug busts in Fort Bragg, my superiors decided it was time to move me to Whitesands Missile Range, New Mexico.

I arrived at Whitesands in April of 1974 and the blanket of dry dessert heat struck me as soon as I stepped of the plane. The drive was forty-five minutes by military bus to the "Range" and was I disappointed. Whitesands appeared so desolate and there was nothing appealing about it. There were no recreational activities on base other than a small movie theater.

The same day I was assigned to the 259th Military Police Company, and while checking into Personnel I discovered that I had the opportunity for an assignment to go anywhere in the world as long as I extended my enlistment for twelve months. I put in a request for an assignment to Presidio of San Francisco, California. After only thirty-five days at the desolate inferno of Whitesands I was extremely happy to leave.

In May 1974, I reported to the 115th Military Intelligence Group, Presidio of San Francisco as my written orders indicated. My verbal orders were to check into the Sixth Region Criminal Investigations Command, San Francisco Field Office, and to a Chief Warrant Officer Robert White. Special Agent White was a tall, large framed black man. He was about six feet, three inches, and about two hundred, and forty-five pounds. His hair line was receding and wore a bushy mustache that didn't comply with Army regulations. He was knowledgeable, and great to work with. He was straight forward and didn't beat around the bush. He told it like it was and didn't candy coat anything. That was fine with me; it's how I preferred it. I didn't like all the added bullshit that comes up in conversations when people try to undermine, and lead others to believe things are different from how they really are.

I went right to work and began scoping out the different areas of the base and kept my ears open. Apparently C.I.D. didn't have much intelligence going for them. Only a few weeks had passed when I hit the mother load. There was a Staff Sergeant in Personnel that had unauthorized possession of United States Army Identification Cards. He was trying to peddle off the cards. I got one from him as a sample and turned it into Chief Warrant Officer White and told him what I knew. The C.I.D. office ran a check on the serial number of the I.D. card and found it was one of two hundred and fifty that were issued to a unit in Viet Nam and had come up unaccounted for. That meant they were either lost or stolen. Being high priority, CID and I had to move fast to recover these cards. If these cards fell into the wrong hands they could be used to commit serious crimes against the United States Army and the United States Government. These cards could get civilians or enemies of the United States onto Military Installations and other potentially sensitive areas. There was just one problem everyone had to take into consideration. Was this I.D. Card incident going to expose me and cripple me from being further effective in the field? Nevertheless, it was a very high priority to recover the I.D. cards before they were distributed, if they hadn't been already. They took the Staff Sergeant down and the two hundred and fifty I.D. cards were all recovered. On December 9,1974 I received my first "Letter Of Commendation".It wasn't awarded in formation in front of the whole company as awards in the Army are normally given. Instead, it was handed to me from Warrant Officer White in a sealed envelope. Nevertheless, when I opened the envelope and read the letter I felt a head rush, and chills running up my spine. That great sense of pride blanketed my entire body. I had done a great service and I felt really good about it (See appendix for copy of letter). Along with great accomplishments sometimes follows pain. I was being reassigned from the 115th Military Intelligence Group to Headquarters and Headquarters Company Garrison. Now somewhat exposed, my Colonel of the 115th (later redesignated 525th) M.I. Group seemed to be upset with me. I suppose it was because I didn't report my status to him. Nevertheless, I hated leaving the 115th because it was a prestigious assignment. I got to drive for the Colonel, got special assignments and did a little traveling to other military bases. Soon I was on my way making contacts and the corroborated information was enough to lead to several big busts. One deal in particular was about to come through with two dealers working as mechanics down at the motor pool. As we got together time and time again to feel each other out, they gave away a little more valuable information about themselves. What was a shocker was that both of them were assigned to Headquarters and Headquarters Company Garrison, my company. My cover story was that I periodically went into Mexico, and smuggled drugs back across the boarder. If anyone ever bothered to check it out there wasn't a problem because my new bride and I would leave San Francisco at least once a month to visit her family down in Fresno. I made up a convincing story that I was tired of making the trip and it was becoming increasingly risky so I was looking for a closer, more convenient supplier, and they were hopefully it. They got excited and I could tell their greed was beginning to get the best of them. I continued to report back to C.I.D. field office and brief them with the updated news. Time was getting very close and I was nearly ready to finalize the deal and go in for the kill. I was going to pounce on these bastards like a tiger pounces on its prey; when he musters that last burst of energy, after a long chase, he leaps, stretches out in complete form, and comes down with complete precision upon its prey. I knew this was going to be a great one. In the meantime, Mr. White had gotten suspended for some unknown reason. I was forced to go the rest of the way with Special Agent Childers. He was a Specialist Sixth Class or E-6. "Bonehead" Childers, as I called him, took me to meet the Narcs at the San Francisco Police Department, Hall Of Justice. I met with several of the Narcs. Let me remind you that this event took place in January 1975. At this point I can only remember two of them by name. I remember Oly, he was a big blonde, middle aged, ruff looking character, and you could tell he was running the show down there. I also meet with Bruce the undercover Narc that I would be working with. We began to exchange information. I was briefed on who, what, how, and how much stuff we would be dealing for. The S.F.P.D. Narcs would provide the buy money and Bruce would hang on to it.

Two days later on Thursday the deal was set for four thirty in the afternoon in the parking lot out in front of Headquarters Company Garrison. That was a great location because the parking lot was huge and always filled with cars. It was perfect for surveillance. Anyone could simply lose themselves in that parking lot and not be detected even if he had the slightest bit of skill in concealment. It was show time! I was sitting in my

blue and white 1974 Plymouth Duster out in the parking lot.
Bruce pulled up in his 1970 beat up Mercury Capri. I got in his
car and we headed for the section in front of HHC Garrison.
I had told our suckers that we would be in a green Mercury
Capri. It was four thirty P.M. and they hadn't showed up. I
looked at my watch. It was 4:45 PM, and still no show. I could
feel they were probably out there somewhere just watching our
every move. Five o'clock came around and I began to wonder
if it was going to happen at all. Bruce had a hand radio stuffed
underneath his seat, but maintained radio silence. Then, out of
the blue, a Honda Celica pulled up in front of us and Dave got
out. He asked if we had the money and we told him,"Ya!" He
wanted to know what we were going to want and I told him I
needed to restock completely and we had plenty of money to
spend so let's get the show on the road because I was tired of
waiting. He told us to follow him and keep up. We darted out
of the base gate and started on our mystery ride. Right turns,
left turns, up streets, down streets, then turns again. Then I
noticed we were headed toward Highway 1, down towards the
beach. Suddenly, he pulled over, got out and asked who was
holding the money. Bruce said he was. Dave decided that he
would get into the Capri with Bruce and take him in to see his
boss, while I went with John his partner who was sitting in the
Toyota Celica. I got into the Celica and, we each speed off in
separate directions. I began to have second thoughts that perhaps this was a rip off or I was about to get myself into some
real serious shit. John was a good size guy and looked like he
was part Oriental. I began to wonder if this asshole knew Karate or something? Nevertheless, Karate or no Karate I was de-
termined to get the slip on this guy and jack him up as soon as
he pulled over. I wasn't about to take any chances. I suddenly
became really concerned and thought to myself; *And where the
hell is my back up*?! I felt that perhaps those jerks had left my
butt hanging out in the wind. Out of nowhere I see this green
piece of junk American Motors Matador trying to pull up on us
and cut us off on the right side I hadn't noticed who it was even
though he was making his move on my side. "Crazy son of a

bitch" I thought. I began to wonder what was going on. In all of the confusion I began to cuss at him because he looked like he was trying to hit us. I finally got a good look at the driver and discovered it was "Bonehead Childers". John pulled over into the Highway One Beach parking lot and jumped on the brakes. Not expecting the outcome he was just as startled as I was. With brakes squealing and smoke coming up in a cloud from the brakes, and tires, Childers and his partner were out and all over us like white on rice. They pulled us both out of the car with guns drawn. Even though I knew I was a good guy and this was my Cavalry I was truly shaken before I could regain control of my senses. They frisked us, cuffed us both and placed us into the back seat of the junky Matador. They searched the suspect vehicle and found paraphernalia in the glove box with residue. They bagged it and took it into custody. They drove us down to the Hall Of Justice. They parked in what seemed to be an underground garage filled with police vehicles both marked and unmarked, and rows and rows of motorcycles. We went up a couple of flights and I remained handcuffed until we each got into our separate and individual interrogation rooms. Once they got me into my individual room they uncuffed me and began the debriefing process. I went over everything that happened in my own words, and then they went through a series of questions. With the suspects secure in their own interrogation rooms I came out with the coast clear and went to the restroom. When I came out Bruce was standing there with a nice cold coke in his hand for me. He congratulated me on a job well done and with a huge smile on his face. He told me to hang loose and make myself at home because he had to get back in there with these clowns. I knew I had done a great job, standing there with a big head enjoying my cold Coke and relieved the worst was over when suddenly a Narc with long nappy hair and a long nasty beard sitting behind a computer began yelling, and at the same time trying to conceal his face. He kept yelling over and over, "Get this guy out of here!" I stood there looking around trying to figure out what, and who this guy was yelling about. Then big Oly came darting out to find out what the commotion was all about. The long haired bum yells out at him "get this guy out of here" pointing at me. Oly got upset and said, "You a------- he's Army CID". There were other undercover Narcs at separate desks busy doing their individual thing and they began to laugh in hysteria. This bum looking Narc saw me enter in cuffs and didn't realize that I was one of the good guys. I tried to keep focused but couldn't help thinking I needed to call my wife and let her know that everything was fine. I didn't want her to be waiting up until late worrying about me. "Hay Bonehead, I need to call home," I blurted out. I grabbed the closest phone and dialed, on the third ring she picked up, "Hello," she said. "Honey it's me, everything went great and everything is fine. I'll be home late." I could tell she was relieved I had made the call. I was just glad to have heard her voice after such a day.

It was already one A.M. I made my way over to a long table and began looking over all of the drugs on it. I wondered where this stuff had come from. A few moments later Childers came over and asked me, "How you like all this shit man?" Saying it with a big smile on his face. I turned and replied, "Someone really hit the jackpot!" Laughing he replied, "You did stupid, this is all from your bust!" I was unbelievably surprised, and began to look at everything closer, but I was careful not to touch. There were many small bundles of marijuana about kilo size. There was a stack of sheets of blotter acid. There were a couple of plastic wrapped packages of a white substance possibly Coke or Heroin I assumed. There was so much it was unreal.

John was in one room, Dave in another, and in a third room had an unknown culprit. The unknown culprit had just gotten out of prison two months earlier for a drug wrap and was out on parole. This unknown culprit was about to go back to prison with some added time to boot. I wondered if he thought it had been worth it all.

It was about three in the morning and I was just getting in. I had to be up by six A.M. and back to work in the Orderly Room like nothing happened. I was tired. It was as if I were holding down two jobs; it was difficult. John and Dave were released to the Provost Marshall on the Presidio. They were now facing criminal charges with the civilian authorities, military charges, and would possibly receive a bad conduct discharge.

Little did I know that this operation involved so much; it took the coordination of multiple agencies. The involvement included, of course, the Army CID, the San Francisco Police Department Narcotics Squad, the United States Customs Service, and the newly formed Drug Enforcement Administration. The big bonus was that there was a bear (helicopter) in the sky to insure that vehicles that were being tracked were not lost in traffic. It made me feel great to know that my "little" drug bust had so much priority. On February 24, 1975 I was at the field office visiting with Bob White, he had just gotten off of suspension and cleared of what ever had happened. Major Crinan, the Field Office Commander, came over to me shook my hand, congratulated me for a job well done, then handed me my second letter of commendation. Chief Warrant Officer White took the letter from me and read it aloud while other agents came in to listen and later congratulated me. It felt great to be recognized and did wonders for my self esteem to know that I had made a difference. Major Crinan later apologized for not being able to award the letters with a military awards ceremony, but I understood that keeping things under wrap was necessary. The letters I received wasn't a lottery win or a medal I could pin on my chest for display, but it was a piece of paper with words written upon it that meant a great deal to me. It made me feel that I was really living up to a standard that I took an oath to uphold. It was the oath I pledged back on August 20, 1971 when I promised to defend the United States against enemies foreign and domestic. I felt if you were selling drugs to my fellow soldiers you were placing national security at risk and you were a domestic enemy of the United States, it was that simple. I attempted to set up more deals, but I was unsuccessful. Presidio was a small installation and small military community aboard it. Word traveled quickly and I was a marked man and no one wanted to talk "dope" with me. On August 13, 1975 I began checking out, my time in the Army was up after four long years. I stopped in at the Field Office to bid my farewells. Mr. White was there and nearly tied me to my seat to try and get me to reenlist. I should have but I was foolish then. It was a great career opportunity. On August 19, 1975 I left the Army that I loved and hated, forever.

CHAPTER 1
THE HIERARCHY

HE WAS RESPONSIBLE for pouring out thousands of pounds of poisonous drugs into the streets of our communities both local and throughout several parts of the United States. Jose was obviously the man in charge. At the age of twenty he stood about five feet eleven inches tall, slim, and with a rich olive clear complexion. Personal appearance was important to Jose. He dressed in the latest fashion of designer clothes, from Versace outer garments to Nike Air Max tennis shoes. His clothes were always neatly pressed and never displayed a sign of wear, as if they had just been taken off the department store clothes rack. He had numerous pairs of shoe wear and neither of them appeared to show signs of aging. Jose had closely cropped hair, and upon his head, never a hair out of place. Jose was always neatly groomed as if he had just left his hair stylist's salon. A mere shadow of hair above his upper lip was the only hint of manhood. Young beautiful women were commonly in his presence. He oozed with sincere boyish charm that won society over as a admired young Mexican man. Jose enjoyed charm, charisma, and power that most young men envy. His brilliant plan was to blend into the community unnoticed. It was an impossible task for one who possessed impeccable qualities that made him stand tall above the crowd. He displayed confidence with every stride he took. At the same time he had this innocence about him that gave people a false sense of trust. Some desired to be in his presence of such a polite and handsome person. Jose also had this remarkable talent to make everyone feel they were important to him. That was powerful talent which served him well in this business; this business of dealing deadly, and illicit drugs. He was a youthful, and handsome twenty year old, the man in charge; the boss of one of the largest drug rings on the west coast. With his pleasant personality, one couldn't help but to like him. This also made him extremely dangerous. He was a chameleon that blended in with your every day common citizen. Little did Jose know that his time was running out and he would soon answer for the evil that he had brought upon society.

Israel was Jose's younger brother. Looking at Israel you could easily mistake him for Jose; with a slightly younger twist. At age eighteen he was well on his way to extreme wealth, or so he thought. He was high up on the food chain only because of his blood relation and not because it had been earned. Israel was responsible for developing and maintaining his own clientele, and assisting in what ever was delegated to him by Jose. Izzy, as he was also known, seemed to be obsessed with his appearance, and how people saw him. He was flashy and in your face with his late model Lexus with gold emblems, and expensive tires and wheels. Flashy sports attire, a thick gold chain hanging around his neck, and gold jewelry did nothing to conceal his line of business. The thick wade of large bills he carried in his pocket attracted attention where ever he went. It made him popular on the high school campus and attracted attention among other students. His clientele were many of the high school teenagers where he attended. He had a following which alleviated any suspicion that he could have ever been lonely. His reckless, and greedy lifestyle would finally contribute to his ultimate demise. He felt like many other young adults; invincible and untouchable even after serious brushes with the law. Within a ten day period he was caught in possession of a .357 caliber hand gun in his car, and was at a friend's home when it got raided with three pounds of Methamphetamine in plain sight on the table. It was obvious to any with common sense that he was being watched closely. Nevertheless, business went on the same as usual, as if everything was fine. His numerous court appearances did nothing to curb his appetite for the dangerous lifestyle that he led.

Daniel at age eighteen, and a high school drop out was Jose's *senior captain*, and closest confidant. He blended in easily in comparison to a contemporary eighteen year old. He kept himself well groomed, but he dressed low key. He liked flashing his wad of money under everybody's nose from time to time. Perhaps this was his way of insuring himself that he and his money hadn't parted company. It was clear that Daniel or "Stud Muffin" as he liked to be called was a heavy weight. He accompanied Jose on almost all of the Mexican business trips that Jose went on. These regular trips were for the purpose of purchasing and arranging the trafficking of drugs across the border into the United States. They specialized in smuggling in large quantities of marijuana, cocaine, and methamphetamine. Daniel often dreamed of taking over the day to day operations of the organization once Jose decided to step down. The events which took place and lead to May 2, 2001 would insure that this would never happen.

Billy Joe, commonly known as BJ, at age twenty was Jose's *junior captain*. He ran a crack house out of Goshen, Ca. He often accompanied Jose to Mexico to assist in the purchasing and smuggling of illicit drugs into the United States. The enterprise of selling Methamphetamine, Marijuana, and Cocaine was BJ's staple. It was uncommon to see him at the main house or in the regular company with Jose. Perhaps it was because BJ was too busy using up the profits keeping himself high on the inventory.

Jessie at age twenty-four was once a close friend, ally, and confidant to Jose. His place on the food chain could be equal of that of a lieutenant before the falling out he had with Jose. Jessie had fallen out of grace with Jose because he had betrayed him in an attempt to make a run on Jose's customers. He had gone around and offered Jose's customers more competitive pricing hoping to put Jose out of business.

It seemed that Jessie had become jealous of the volume of business Jose was doing. Jessie was known within the organization as "Fat Ass" this was a name Jose had given to him much before I came on the scene. At approximately six feet, four inches, and weighing in at about a whopping three hundred and thirty-five pounds the name suited him. Besides the wade of money Jessie carried with him at all times the only thing distinct about him was his size and the fact that he wore the same clothes for days on end. Anyone could guess what Jessie had eaten nearly all week long; all you had to do is look at the food stains on his shirt. He must have thought that there was a laundry soap shortage. It wouldn't be long before Jessie would betray Jose, and it nearly cost him his life.

Alexander at age twenty-one stood about five feet, eight inches tall, and weighed in at about one hundred and fifty pounds. He kept a shaved head and chose to wear fashionable clothes and his choice of colors were black on black. Alex was a colorful character with a likable personality, and he was always laughing, and joking about something. Although Alex had his own clientele he worked directly for Jessie as his errand boy. It was obvious that Alex was going nowhere fast because Jessie was selfish, greedy, and would see to it that Alex continued to be dependant upon him. Alex didn't even rate within Jose's hierarchy except that he was a friend and business associate. His loyalty remained with Jessie although he was well aware of the influence, and violence Jose could muster.

Christopher at twenty years old became Jose's errand boy, and ran one of his crack houses. He was coming up quickly in a financial sense and made sure those around him knew it. In a very short time he went from having nothing to acquiring a newer late model red Hyundai, wearing gold jewelry, and wearing flashy clothing normally associated with gang members. Chris, or Goober as he was sometimes called, continued to operate Jose's crack house on Excelsior Ave. He ran errands until he established his own clientele and was able to move on. Goober was a soft spoken, likable person that had always maintained a respectable demeanor towards me. He came from a well known respectable family, and it's a down right shame that he got caught up in this drug culture of destruction.

Goober finally left being Jose's errand boy and ventured out to expand on his enterprising abilities. When it was all over the authorities had him on other charges. Apparently he had transported drugs across county lines and was busted making a sale to undercover narcotics officers. He then tried to deny his involvement and claimed the officers had planted the evidence, and had taken part of the money for the purchase. He had racked up a bunch of extra bonus points towards hard time in the big house. It really stunk to be him.

Arthur came in and took over Goober's place. After going a long time without a nickname, Jose finally dubbed him, Furbee. At age nineteen, he was already playing in the major leagues. He stood at about six feet tall, of medium build, and was a simple individual, never flashing what he had. He began first earning a measly fifty dollars a day for all that he had at risk. Furbee somehow later was able to convince Jose to increase his daily wages to one hundred dollars a day. Furbee was a simple, and weak minded individual, and it wouldn't take much to get him to tell all about Jose's operation once he was experiencing the confines of an interrogation room with an FBI Agent at the helm. On May 2, 2001 Furbee would be singing a more beautiful tune than Pavarotti could have at one of his performing operas.

There were numerous players within this organization that significantly contributed to the financial success and dominance that will be mentioned on, in this publication. As of today there have been seventy-three arrests. One defendant was acquitted on state narcotics charges, seventy defendants have plead out and are serving time in either State or Federal Prison. One defendant who decided to go to trial was found guilty on all charges and received ten years in State Prison. One defendant was placed into the California Witness Protection and is tucked away safely for his assistance and testimony. Three co-conspirators are on the run and believed to be hiding in Mexico. Many of the defendants cooperated with authorities which lead to even more arrests. This sweep of arrests was the largest in the history of Kings County and one of the largest in the history of the State of California. Not so much for the volume of drugs, weapons, and drug money recovered, but for the number of people arrested in the sweep. Adding on to those arrested were the others which had been snitched on. Many of the rats had worked their way out of the wood work making deals with authorities so that they could save themselves. By the time they had either all pled out, or gone to trial there were still a number of them still wanted.

CHAPTER 2
METHL SULFONYL METHANE

IT WAS A HOT Sunday in August when the business line of my telephone rang. "Hay Tony, what's up? I want to know if you would open up the store for a very good friend of mine who's interested in buying a 125 gallon aquarium, and all the filters and stuff that he'll need?" Joe inquired. "Go ahead and bring him over. I'll be waiting." was my reply.

Joe was a regular customer with an open credit account. He had bought two aquariums from me in the past and had referred several very good customers to me who had purchased large tanks, with all the fixings, and fish.

I was in the house watching television waiting for Joe and his friend to arrive when the dogs began to bark. It was my cue that someone again wanted me to open my combination farm, feed, and pet store. I looked out the window, and sure enough it was Joe and his friend, a prospectively new customer. I walked out from the house, across the asphalt, opened the store, and let them in. Since it was Sunday we were closed but occasionally I would open up for customers who had an emergency or special need.

Joe introduced us, "Tony this is Mike, Mike this is Tony." We both shook hands while Joe continued, "Mike is a very god friend of mine, we went to school together, and we hang out. He wants a tank for salt water fish and you're the best guy to see." I went through the total sales pitch, explained his options for filtration and other accessories did a price comparison on the various costs and allowed him to decide what he wanted.

Mike decided he wanted a saltwater set up. He purchased a 125 gallon tank, canopy, stand, and all the fixings. His retail purchase totaled approximately two thousand dollars. I had hoped that this sale was all cash but nevertheless, I opened up a credit account for him on Joe's agreement to be responsible for the debt if Mike failed to pay. Mike placed seven hundred down and the balance was carried on the account. I explained to Mike, "Payment due every month, no later than the 5th of the month, and each payment is two hundred dollars, is that alright?" Mike agreed and signed the invoice. My son and I loaded up the tank onto my pick up truck, delivered it, and set it up in Mike's home. Mike seemed to be a really nice person. He stood about six feet, dark complexion, scarred from acne, and well groomed short hair. He was self employed and operated a lawn and garden business. He seemed to be a hard working, tax paying asset to society. Little did I know that his lawn business was a front for his drug business and he was really known as Caesar. I found out later that he was big time. It made sense to me because of the company he kept and the suspicious activity going on I noticed while we delivered and set up his tank. People were trafficking in, coming and going. They would whisper to each other and exchange money for something small that was placed into their hands. To talk to him, one would never know that he was in the big league dealing large volumes of Methamphetamine locally, into the Fresno area, and across state lines. His operation consisted of a few mules (mules are those that are at a lower level working for someone else with the control). He liked doing a lot of the wheeling and dealing. He owned a few nice vehicles: a restored 1970 Cadillac, a late model Mercury Cougar, an Infinity Q45, and a nice Chevy pickup truck he used for his lawn service. All but the pickup had expensive tires, wheels, and each with an expensive stereo system in them. I was told that the stereo system in the Cadillac cost him eight thousand dollars. It wasn't long before my business began to significantly increase. I noticed a significant increase in foot traffic, aquarium supply sales, and especially in the horse supplement product we carried called

MSM (Methl SulfonylMethane). We first began carrying this product in one pound plastic jars and found they didn't stay on the shelf for very long. People were coming in and purchasing several at a time. I decided that we would start stocking the two pound containers and order a few more jars than we normally had. The MSM sales continued to increase at a surprising rate and had difficulty keeping the shelves stocked. It wasn't long before we had graduated into the four pound size, and we began to receive requests for the ten pound size. We phased out the one pound, and two pound containers completely because they were no longer practical.

MSM is the abbreviation for Methl Sulfonyl Methane an ingredient which is found in all foods, but not in high quantities to properly provide for ones daily needs. MSM is used to supplement one's diet to maintain one's joints, and alleviate pains throughout parts of the body. The product was first introduced, and marketed for race horses. This product claimed to induce a better and faster recovery, and repair of cells that were damaged, or torn down due to heavy training performance periods. Soon, this product was then introduced as a supplement for humans. What I didn't know at the time was that drug dealers were using MSM to cut or dilute the potency of pure Methamphetamine down to street marketable potencies. Little did it I know that most of the MSM I sold was being sold for "Meth". When I did find out I became angry that I was being used by profiteering "Ballers" (drug dealers). I thought back about my cousin and the adverse effects that dangerous drugs had on her, and her destruction. I thought about my comrades-in-arms I had served with in the Army the drugs had destroyed. I began to give the situation a lot of thought and felt that I had to do something. First, we raised the price of the MSM to make it unattractive for them to purchase, and that didn't work. It came to the point where the price of the MSM was outrageous and it continued to sell regardless of the price. I felt I wasn't doing enough and I had to do more. I decided to penetrate Jose's organization, and gather as much information as I could about them. The second step would be to contact the Drug Enforcement Administration and notify them of what I was about to learn. I felt I had to gather enough convincing information in order to get them to act appropriately and not ignore this serious problem.

It was on a Sunday morning at about seven A.M. the dogs began to bark and the door bell rang. I looked out the window and it was Rudy. Rudy was a regular customer that came into the store almost weekly to buy MSM. I went to the door, opened it and there was Rudy and standing with him was another young man who he introduced as Jose. Rudy purchased about six pounds, paid me cash, and off he went. I began to closely monitor the MSM sales. Jose began to come over on Sunday morning like clock work. He purchased anywhere from four to six pounds at a time. There were times where he would come over twice on a Sunday. The MSM business obviously became very lucrative for us. It wasn't my intention to benefit greatly from the sales of MSM to drug dealers, it happen by chance. The ten pound buckets finally became the most popular of all the sizes. Our cost on a ten pounder was $67.50 and we were charging $450.00 each. To our legitimate customers that would purchase it for their horse we would charge them $100.00 which was a fair mark up.

Jose continued to come over on Sunday mornings, and I assumed it was because he thought that it was safer to operate on Sundays, and free from the watchful eye of law enforcement. He was probably right, for the most part. He spent increasingly more time in my office with me talking about his personal life and things that interested him. I began to like him as a person and at times could easily see what I had to do was going to be hard. I couldn't allow my emotions to interfere with what had to be done. After all I had to think of the innocent children that were adversely affected by what he was doing. What about the families that were being deprived, and neglected because one or both parents had a drug dependency from the drugs Jose was placing onto the streets? What about the unborn, who awaited birth but were already addicted because their mothers were dependant and using during the pregnancy? How much would those innocent unborn suffer in agony with dependencies of their own, and disabilities? In the least the burden society would carry to try, and correct this behemoth indignity, and all the ramifications that would follow. Those thoughts converted from like to dislike for Jose and drove me forward to accomplish what I had set out to do.

On one occasion on a Sunday morning in my office Jose asked, "You know a lot of people don't you?" I replied, "Yes I do, and why is that?" Jose replied, "Well if you ever want to get into the business of selling Meth, Cocaine, Marijuana, or Ecstasy let me know. I'll teach you all you need to know about the business, and I'll set you up." My next question was, "How much for Meth by the pound?" Jose, "A pound of Meth cut is $3,000.00 and purity is $7,000.00 a pound. I concluded the conversation with I'll think about it and let you know should I decide. Jose began to entrust me more and he began to call on short notice to have me deliver MSM to different locations. Therefore, I began to carry two ten pound MSM in the back of my pickup truck just in case he called. I felt I had enough to move on Jose and notify the DEA or some other agency. I had to give it some thought on how I wanted to do it. It turned out I never had to make the decision; they came to me. It was mid August 2000 and three FBI Agents arrived at my store. They had located two receipts at Cesear's house during a search and traced them back to me. They questioned my wife and, I extensively about Cesear's purchases and Joe's receipt. Unaware that the FBI was investigating drug related offenses surprised me. After a couple of hours of answering their questions they each left me their cards and left.

I had long decided that I wasn't about to work with local law enforcement because I didn't trust them. Seven years prior, on July 14, 1993 at one A.M., three seventeen year old male gang members invited themselves over to my place with criminal intentions with more detail on their minds. My fifteen year old son and I held them down at gun point until the Sheriff's Deputies arrived after my wife called 911. These three were responsible for barraging my home with hundreds of threatening, and harassing phone calls. The Sheriff's Office had been called out numerous times and nothing was ever done to stop it. The actions of these three delinquents stemmed from a law suit I had entered against a business competitor of mine. This competitor had hired these three to make my life miserable through fear, and intimidation. On approximately July 28 my home was raided by the Sheriff's Deputies in search of weapons. Two weeks later arrest warrants were issued for my son, wife, and I. Charges were dropped against my wife at the preliminary stage. I was bound over for trial and was acquitted of all the charges. My son's charges were dismissed in the interest of just the following week after my acquittal. We later sued Kings County in Superior Court under Federal Civil Rights Statutes and won a judgment against the Deputy responsible for $50,000.00. The other half of the law suit was to be tried at a later date against the former District Attorney for his part in the malicious prosecution. The county offered us an additional $75,000.00 to settle that portion of the case. This judgment was barely enough to cover the costs of the criminal trial and the civil suit. As a result of both trials the Sheriff's Office had immense animosity for me instead of the Deputy who was responsible for bringing this all about. I had plenty of reason not to place my life in their hands.

Elections had come around and Kings County had a new Sheriff and new District Attorney. For the next four years the Sheriff's Office and the District Attorney's Office would battle it out over numerous issues. Apparently the Sheriff had a great desire to control the DA's Office and the struggle continued. The new DA was a good and moral man, and his desire to do the right, and ethical thing drove him. His term as DA lasted only one term (four years) and he was replaced by another who was endorsed by the Sheriff. The Sheriff a master in the political arena flexed his political and influential power within the community, and had the former DA defeated in the elections.

The news that the FBI was in town and nosing around in my business had spread like the plague. In a matter of hours members of the local drug culture were asking me about their inquiries. It was obvious that it was more than just curiosity they were nervous. Of course I couldn't deny that I had contact with them in my store so I played it off and told everyone who asked that I had told them nothing. I waited approximately two weeks for things to cool down and decided it was now time to make my move. I contacted a Special Agent from the FBI who I'll call "Big Bird". He was at the shooting range and told me he would call me back as soon as he was finished there. An hour passed and my cell phone rang it was him. We agreed to meet at the Kings County Law Library. He showed up with another Agent named Julio. We left almost immediately and drove to Lyon's Restaurant where I had a glass of ice tea and they had their late lunch. We discussed a few things and were careful that no one overheard the conversation. When they finished their lunch and my ice tea we all left the parking lot in my Expedition. I took them to the different locations that I had delivered MSM to and had seen large quantities of drugs. Our tour concluded and we went our separate ways.

A week had passed and I received a telephone call from "Big Bird" asking me to come up to the Fresno Office and the conversation went as follows: "Tony this is "Big Bird" I was wondering if you could come up to the Fresno Office and meet with myself and another agent?" In response, "Sure I'll come up is tomorrow alright, about one o'clock?" We agreed and he proceeded to give me directions. I had asked if it was secluded and not an obvious, and known location. He assured me it was secluded, and not an obvious location. I didn't want my truck seen in an FBI parking lot or seen coming or going from an FBI building. Obviously if discovered in the process it could have been deadly.

It was Tuesday and I was on my way to Fresno to meet with "Big Bird" and another Agent I will call "Kellogg". I arrived in the parking lot and was pleased to see that it was huge, and filled with several hundred vehicles, my pickup would blend in perfectly and go unnoticed. The building was large with several stories and with no identifying marks or signs indicating that the FBI occupied office space there. I felt more at ease that the possibility of some bad guys being out in the parking lot and watching to see who came and went was nil. I made my way into the elevator and went up to the prospective floor, walked down the hallway, and entered the door. I announced myself to the receptionist and moments later "Big Bird" opened a door which was protected by a metal detector. I walked through and took a seat at the table. "Big Bird" offered me something to drink and I accepted a cold coke. The room was small with one small table, but large enough to accommodate four people comfortably with four chairs. The room was noticeably divided by an adjustable wall. "Big Bird" took a seat opposite me and to my left, and Kellogg came into the room and took a seat directly opposite where I was sitting. I felt the purpose for the meeting was to feel me out. Of course they had already checked me out locally. I assumed that they would have conducted an extensive back ground investigation on me. If I had been in their shoes I would have gathered as much information as possible on someone I was interviewing. They knew about the law suits and the event which occurred in 1993 with those three "gang bangers". Kellogg" opened up the conversation with questions, "Why do you want to help us, are you looking to go into the witness protection program, and how do we know that you're not Mr. Hanford Drug Dealer looking to use us to eliminate your competition?" I responded as nicely as I could feeling insulted, "First, I want to help you because I don't like what is going on. It's in your face drug dealing all over Hanford and the cops aren't doing enough to eradicate the problem. They're taking the street corner dealers off the street but they're not going after the "king pins", Hanford has become a drug haven for the drug dealer and it's got to change." I continued, "Furthermore, I'm not looking to go into the "Witness Protection Program", but I would like to keep the option open if it is really necessary." Feeling frustrated I went on. "Look, you guys already know that I'm not a drug dealer, you should have already checked me out, and you know that I've done this type of work before while in the military. I probably want to help you guys more than you want me, but that's alright as long as we can get the job done." Kellogg snapped back at me. "How much ephedrine were you supplying Jose with?" I suppose that question was thrown at me to get a rise out of me. I was extremely insulted with the question and responded, "I don't know where you're getting your information from but you better check out your source. Jose was getting his ephedrine from some middle easterners is what he told me." "Big Bird" kept silent for the most part, but I felt he was more anxious to work with me than "Kellogg". Kellogg finally brought up the issue of selling the MSM, "Didn't you know that these guys were utilizing the MSM for illegal purposes?" I felt as though he was trying to make me feel like I had done something wrong, "First, I must say that it is none of my business what people do with the products they buy from me once they pay for them and go out the door. I'm not obligated to inquire, interrogate, or discriminate. I didn't know what they were doing until just recently, and kept them on the wire for the purpose of notifying federal law enforcement. My intention was to contact the DEA and work with them, but you guys were already involved. If you guys don't want to work with me that is alright I'll just go see them with what I have." "Big Bird" responded with, "We're not saying we're not interested." I continued on, "MSM is an over the counter product which is widely sold to the open public, easily accessible so if there is a problem with it then the government needs to take measures to curtail its sales." I knew the interview was just a formality, and a normal process. I concluded the meeting with, "I want to make it perfectly clear that if we do decided to work with each other than I don't want the locals to know what I'm doing. I don't trust them. If and when the time comes where they have to be told then you let me know." We shook hands, bid our good byes, and I was on my way. On the way home I didn't give the meeting much more thought. I really didn't care what they were thinking after all I knew I was the "golden goose" I could get the desperately needed results.

A week went by and I received a telephone call from "Big Bird", "We would like you to come back up to Fresno and meet with the assistant U.S. Attorney tomorrow at ten A.M. Is that good for you?" I responded, "Yes, that will work just fine. I'll be there. Is it the same building where you're at?" "Big Bird", "No the meeting will be down at the Federal Building in downtown Fresno." I acknowledged I knew where it was and we hung up.

The following day I met with the FBI and the Assistant U.S. Attorney I'll call "Julian". The meeting went really well and it was brief. After our brief discussion "Big Bird" and "Kellogg" shook hands and welcomed me to the team. In leaving I felt the need to share what had transpired with someone because I couldn't go home and talk about it with my family. I called a good friend of mine in law enforcement and we met over coffee later that evening. He praised me for my courage and said I was doing a great community service.

The next day I called my son who's an Army Officer and told him he needed to keep quiet. I didn't totally trust the FBI. Things could go bad during this operation and they may not accept responsibility for any possible mistakes, and then try to make me look like I was dirty. I just wasn't sure and I needed a safety net in place just in case. I began to have second thoughts and wondered if these guys were going to look out for me. Only time would tell, and I was anxious to get the ball rolling.

CHAPTER 3
CODE NAME COLUMBUS

THERE WAS AN agreement between "Kellogg", "Big Bird", and myself that the locals would not be informed of my roll in this investigation until it came a time that it was absolutely necessary. It was also agreed upon that when that time came we would discuss it or in the least I would be told. During the entire investigation I continued to ask, "Do the locals know the status of my involvement or have you told them anything?" Each time "Kellogg" and "Big Bird" denied that the locals knew anything.

A few days after our meeting with Assistant United States Attorney Julian had taken place I was issued a code name. I was briefed as to how and why this code name would be used. Kellogg said, "I selected a code name that would suit you." With a suspicious expression I asked, "Oh and what name would that be?" Kellogg, "I selected Columbus. How do you like it?" I said, "Why in the world Columbus?" Kellogg answered, "Well Columbus was a great Portuguese explorer and you're Portuguese so it's perfect, Columbus." I laughed sarcastically, "What are you, stupid? Don't you know your history? Listen up and I'll give you a quick history lesson: Columbus was Italian and flew under the Spanish flag for the Queen of Spain who financed his exploration to the new world, of which he was really searching for a shorter route to bring back spices." He began to argue with a facial expression filled with doubt. I added to the insult, "You must have been asleep during that lesson in the fourth grade right? I guess they'll hire anyone in the FBI." From this point on any time they referred to me in written reports or speak of me they were supposed to use the code name Columbus.

Columbus had taken on a very difficult task that would last nine months. My involvement would have to be kept secret from my family including my wife. My wife distrusted law enforcement completely. Keeping it from her was two fold. First, she didn't trust law enforcement and rightfully so after the incident of 1993. There was a strong possibility that she would not have allowed me to go on. Secondly, there was always a possibility that she could slip in casual conversation which would create a serious problem. As time went on we began to argue about my activities, the company I kept, and the people I was dealing with. The calls I would receive late at night and have to get up, and leave after already being bedded down for the night. Our relationship continued to be strained, and the level increased as I got in deeper. The children were becoming disrespectful making comments that they suspected I was in bad business and company. I could tell that they weren't happy what appeared to them I was doing. I had to act like I was a hood when I was around the "friendly neighborhood drug dealer" and had to keep my guard up when at home and around my family. I had given this project a lot of thought and consideration before I began, and knew it was going to be difficult, and it was.

CHAPTER 4
THE OPERATION BEGINS

I COMMUNICATED ALMOST daily with "Big Bird" and "Kellogg", and updated them on current trends and changes with our subjects. They instructed me to set up a four pound buy of methemphetamine from Jose. Jose wanted $3,000.00 a pound for his meth, what he normally charged everyone else. Although it was government money I didn't feel that I should be giving this bastard any more money than I really had to. I certainly didn't want to feed into his operation. I was under no pressure by the Bureau to negotiate a price, but I thought it good business, and an obligation to the taxpayers after all, it is their money. Jose and I met at his residence at Galileo to fine tune the deal. Opening up the negotiations I said, "Jose, I realize you want $3,000.00 a pound for the Meth. In consideration of the potential volume I can move for you, I'll give you $2,800.00 a pound." It surprised me that he agreed without any further discussion, Jose was fine with it, "Sure, no problem, it's a deal." I felt that perhaps I hadn't negotiated well enough and should have gone lower.

It was my job to select a rally point for the operation, somewhere secluded would be appropriate. I chose the old Sagrabella's abandoned residence on ninth avenue out in the country. It was perfect: secluded and plenty of shade. It was eight A.M. and time for the recorded call to be made. I called and a voice came on, "Tony Montana, I'll be ready in a little bit. Give me some time and I'll call you back; I'm just getting up." I replied, "Yeah, OK, I don't want this shit taking all f_____

day man!" "No, no, it won't for sure man!" confirmed Jose. So
we sat and waited. Little did Jose know that he was under close
surveillance, and every move of his was being closely watched.
We waited and waited, lunch time came around, and one of the
other agents made a Mac Donald's run into town, he came back
and we continued to wait. We ate our lunch and small talked
under the big shade tree and the clock ticked. In the mean time,
Jose had already left for his crack house on Excelsior Avenue.
That residence was under close surveillance. Finally the call
that we had all been waiting for came. My cell phone was ringing and looking at the sight glass I could see it was coming up
Jose. Jose, "Tony Montana everything is ready for you but I
won't be there, you'll pick up from Goober." I replied, "Hay
son of -----! I don't like that shit! I want to deal directly with
you!" Jose, "No, it's cool. He's my cousin and you've met him
before, you know him, it's Goober." I said, "OK man, I don't
want any funny shit. I want it smooth." It was beautiful, the
recorder was on, and we got it all. My pickup truck had already
been thoroughly searched along with my person, and belong-
ings. This is a common procedure when doing a "controlled
buy". This is done to protect the parties involved, and the
integrity of the buy itself. The defense can't later come back
and say that he was framed, and the evidence drugs were not
purchased from his client. I signed for the $11,200.00 in cash
with the endorsement Columbus. Then they strapped me with a
wire. I was totally against going in with a wire, but that's what
they wanted me to do. They knew full and well that if they
decided to shake me down I was screwed and possibly dead.
For sure the "jig" would be up and these jerks would continue
on with their drug enterprise. All I could think about was how
unsophisticated and primitive the FBI really was. I had worn
a wire back in the early nineteen seventies, and I couldn't believe we hadn't evolved into something more advanced, and
less risky. There was almost enough wire throughout my body
that I could have wired up my television set up to the roof of
my house. The shit was bad, and I was getting bad vibes, but
I did it anyways to demonstrate that I was sincere about it all.

I would have to remain conscious that I was wired up and to avoid any physical contact that might give me away. It was show time. I was on my way to Jose's crack house on Excelsior Avenue and on my way there, I turned on my compact disc player and put on Carlos Santana's "Smooth". Just as the saying goes, "music calms the savage beast", in this case the savage beast was my nerves. I had finally arrived, I pulled onto the dirt driveway, and there was a late model red Hyundai parked beside the house. I described the vehicle aloud, and read off the license plate number so the wire picked up and transmitted the information back. I left the money in the glove box wrapped in a brown paper bag while I went inside just in case they decided to rip me off. I said, "Hay you got my shit, is it, I don't want any junk." Goober replied, "It's good man." The Meth was in an empty ten pound MSM bucket. I had him take it out and place the Meth into a bag. "How many we got here? It should be a full four pounds here. You're not shorting me, are you?" " No, no, it's all here guaranteed" he reassured me. "OK one, two, three, four, super." I had him pick up the dope and place it into the bag so I would be sure to get his prints on it. I then told him, "I'll be right back I'm getting the cash out of my truck."Going out and getting the money was an indicator to my back up that I had seen the dope and everything was going fine. I headed back inside with the cash and began to lay out the money in piles of one thousand dollars and counting it aloud so the wire again picked up on it and transmitted it back. As I laid out the first pile he went to pick it up and I told him wait until I was completely through counting. I finished and told him to count it all out, and when he finished I asked if it was all there, the whole eleven thousand, two hundred dollars. He replied, "Yep!" My justification to him, "I just wanted to make sure there are no mistakes and no questions later." He responded, "That's cool." I went through the whole verbal procedure because I wanted to make sure we had a clear record, and I didn't want there to be ant doubts of who was doing what, and how much was being exchanged. The transaction had concluded and I was on my way out the door and to my truck, and relieved that everything had gone so well. Driving back to the rally point I was followed by several surveillance vehicles. Throughout the drive back surveillance back up units would break off while others would pick up on me. This procedure was conducted so that it didn't breach the integrity of the controlled buy, and protected me and the drugs from a potential rip off. After all there hadn't been any buys until now and we didn't know what Jose's intentions were whether to conduct a bonafide transaction or set up for a rip off. While listening to a refreshing Santana tune I arrived onto the rally point and parked with Kellogg and Big Bird right behind, and the surveillance vehicle right behind them. Kellogg immediately took possession of the drugs. I went through the thorough search process all over again, and of course everything cleared. Again that was done so that the defense couldn't accuse me of being dirty, and have picked up drugs for myself. I went through the debriefing process and filled Kellogg in on what was said and transpired. The recording would verify all that had occurred.

Monday had passed and the "wire experience" was still fresh on my mind. I wondered how many stupid things they were going to have me do that would place me into unnecessary danger. After giving the issue of wearing the wire much thought I had decided I wouldn't take that foolish risk again. They were going to have to come upwith something else.

Tuesday I called Jose from my home and recorded the conversation. After he answered I said, "Jose, this is Tony, everything is cool, it's good stuff. I need another big one for Thursday morning," Jose, "Hay Montana, I'll have it ready for you just call me Thursday morning." Jose chose to call me Tony Montana because he said I reminded him of Al Pacino in the movie "Scarface". Jose liked giving people nick names, I suppose I made out better than Jessie did after all he had to live with "Fat Ass".

Thursday morning arrived and we all met at the rally point. All were present just as before. Kellogg and Big Bird went through the normal procedures of searching my pick up truck and person. I made the call and Jose answered, "Tony Montana, I'm just getting up, I've got to get to the shower and then I'll call you back, I had a long night." Tony, "Hay Jose, I don't want this shit to take all day like last time. I've got people waiting and they're not going to wait all day!" Jose replied, "No, it won't take all day, I'll call you back."

We waited there at the rally point and to pass the time Big Bird and I small talked while Kellogg monitored, and listened on the radio. Transmissions were coming over the air periodically about Jose's movement. There was activity going on over at the Excellsior Avenue crack house that Jose had rented from a local dairyman. The electronics surveillance agent walked over to me, and said, "I've got some bad news for you Tony we won't be using the wire that we used last time anymore. We have information that Jose uses police scanners to monitor police transmissions. If in fact he is using a scanner while you go in with a wire, the scanner will transmit and amplify the conversation your having with him as you speak. At that moment I had a mixed feeling of anxiety, nervousness, and relief come over me all at once. My first thought was shit! I wore a wire last time what if he had a scanner on then? Man these guys were screwing up big time! Nevertheless, I got over that feeling, and I became relieved about the whole wire issue. I was never going to wear one again. As those other feelings passed I became angry. How could these idiots have screwed up so bad. This could have been the end of the beginning not only for the operation but for me.

It was about 9:30 A.M. and, the radio call came over the air from the surveillance team. Jose was on the move and had arrived at the Excellsior crack house. At 10:30 A.M. Jose called. Jose, "Montana everything is ready, and waiting." Tony, "I'm on my way."

We hadn't yet discussed what I was going to use as a recording device, when the agent pulled out a neat little toy. It appeared to be a beeper, it didn't have the capability to transmit it could only record. I liked it and it looked inconspicuous. One thing I didn't like about it was that it didn't have the functions of a beeper. It was only cosmetic. Kellogg activated the recorder, and I was on my way with plenty of back up and cover. I took the exact same path as before, turned on the CD player, and tuned it in to Santana. I needed something "smooth" to calm the air, and something sleek to slow down the heat beat. As the tune "Maria, Maria" began, I began to relax, and aloud I spate out, "This one is for you "Big Bird!" I did it to be comical, and catch them off guard when they reviewed the recorded tape. Down Ninth Avenue, left on Houston Avenue to Fourteenth Avenue, and then right, through the tiny town of Armona. As I was coming up on Flint Avenue my cell phone rang. It was Big Bird, " Tony, Jose is just up ahead on Fourteen Avenue talking to some guys parked on the side of the road take a detour." I responded, "OK got you covered!" I immediately took a left onto Flint Avenue. I understood that if I ran into Jose it would create problems. First, Jose would spot my tail with Kellogg and Big Bird in it. Secondly there was no one else covering them in case they lost visual contact with me; it would have created problems for the integrity of the controlled buy. Losing sight of me at any time other than when I went in for the transaction would invalidate the buy. I then took a right on Fourteen and one half, then left onto Excelsior Avenue, and I pulled right into the dirt drive where there were vehicles none of which were familiar to me except the red Hyundai. I began to read off the license plates, and vehicle makes aloud so that it was all clearly recorded. As I attempted to go into the house someone else was coming out. I made a mental note of his physical description, and Goober met me at the door as I entered. They were definitely open for business today. I saw a cardboard flat from a 24-case of canned soda filled with plastic wrapped bundles of what appeared to be Cocaine, Meth, and Marijuana. They were stacked as if placed, and organized to be picked up for individual orders.

Same as before, I left the money in my glove box. Goober took out the one pound of an off white colored substance wrapped up tightly in plastic in a cylindrical shape same as before. The distinct aroma of fresh Meth filled the air. An indescribable smell that was pleasant, not foul, but yet like no other odor I could compare to. I had Goober take it out and place it back into the bag so I was sure to get his prints on the packaging. The conversation went like this: I said, "Is there a full pound here? Goober replied, "Yep it's all there." In response I said, "Sure smells fresh." Goober replied, "We just got done making it last night." Curiously I asked, "How much I owe you, twenty-eight hundred, right?"

I went out and retrieved the money from the glove box just as I had the last time. I came back and began to lay out the money in one thousand dollar stacks, the last stack containing eight one hundred dollar bills. While I counted aloud Goober stood by and watched. I then told him to pick up the money and count it. I asked, "All there?" Goober answered. "Yep, be cool. Later." I concluded with, "Yep later."

I made my way to my pick up truck, and someone else had pulled up and was making their way to the door. As I passed him, I again made a mental note of his physical appearance. Eye contact was not made as he passed me by as if I were invisible. I got into my pickup and headed back to the Rally Point the same exact route as I had taken to get there. As I watched in my rear view mirror I was suddenly alerted. Someone was following me that didn't look familiar to me. I got on my cell phone and called Kellogg, gave him the description of the vehicle, and person inside from what I could see. Kellogg reassured me it was one of ours. As I arrived at the Rally Point a vehicle following me went down a little further, turned around, pulled over, and watched me as I waited for Kellogg and Big Bird to arrive. As they arrived the mystery vehicle speed away. My pickup was again searched along with my person. Kellogg took immediate possession of the Meth and placed it into a bag, documented the description, time, and date. Kellogg then took possession of the recording device and shut it off. I was then debriefed, and instructed to set up another buy for tomorrow for one and a half pounds. I called Jose and told him everything was great, and ordered another one and a half pounds of Meth for tomorrow all the while recording the conversation.

Finally Friday rolled in and we all gathered at the usual Rally

Point. The routine began all over again, the search, the briefing, and reviewing the procedures. I began to call Jose but he wasn't picking up. Finally at ten A.M. Jose called. Jose: "Montana, I couldn't call you earlier because Israel had his court hearing today. I was tied up at the hearing. He's coming home. Give me a little time to get things ready. I'll call you back." In reply I said, "OK, I got people waiting. Don't take all day." I already knew where he was, and what he was doing. We had people following him and people at the court house watching, and listening. The Bureau already knew Israel had a court date. They filled me in while they briefed me.

We continued to wait, and finally decided I would just go over there. We knew Jose had finally made his way to the crack house on Excelsior. The Surveillance Team had already reported movement over the radio in to Kellogg. Kellogg then alerted the team that we were on the move. I placed the activated recording device on me. I pulled out and began to travel the same route that I had traveled the other times before. As I approached Excelsior I could see Jose's red Dodge pickup truck just crawling east bound on Excelsior Avenue. I thought if I can see his truck he can likely see mine. I looked at my rear view mirror and could see the FBI vehicle not too far behind me. Looked like a typical cop car. A lot of things began to go through my mind at this point, but I just prayed everything was alright, and nothing alerted him, or gave him any ideas. At this point I had wished that I had become invisible to him. I had hoped that he hadn't made Kellogg's car. In the meantime I had slowed down, and had tapped my breaks to alert Kellogg, and allowing Jose to hopefully get out of sight. I again pulled onto the dirt driveway at the Excelsior crack house, and parked. I proceeded to the house while the money remained in my glove box. As I approached the rear entrance I noticed a blonde male appearing to be looking over a moped parked under the back patio to the house. Goober opened the back door as I went to knock. He must have been watching. I went inside and on the counter there was a cardboard flat same as last time with plastic wrapped packages neatly arranged as if waiting to be picked up. Goober had the one and one half pounds set aside and ready for me. One cylindrical one pound size, and another wrapped up the same way, but half the size of the larger one. Goober broke silence with, "It's all here one and a half pounds." I replied, "I'm short of cash so I'll just take a half pound." Goober in response, "That's fine." I counted out the fourteen hundred dollars in stacks as I normally did, and counted aloud to get it on the recorder. I then demanded, "Count it out and make sure it's all there." He responded, "Jose just finished up with this batch this morning." I replied, "How good is it compared to the other stuff?" Goober then reassured me and said, "it's better, he prepared this one special for you." I proceeded out the door, and the blonde guy was still outside looking over the moped. I got into my pickup truck and drove onto the roadway, and began to retrace my way back to the Rally Point. I could see the unmarked car containing Kellogg, and Big Bird driving a short distance behind me. I reached the Rally Point, pulled in, and everyone else began to pull in right behind me. Kellogg got out of his car, took immediate possession of the recording device. He checked in the Meth and placed it into his car. We began the debriefing process, and that concluded the days work for me. For the next several months we remained stagnant without making any further buys, but there was still much work that had to be done. I still continued to gather, and provide valuable intelligence that would identify other players within the organization. Bits and pieces of information continued to roll in building an air tight case against these in despicable bunch of undesirable human beings.

Jose expected his customers to be loyal, and purchase all of their drugs from him. A lot of Jose's time was taken up between trips to Mexico, and Arkansas. The Mexico trips were justified because he needed to negotiate pricing for the illicit drugs, and the planning, and strategy he would use to deceive United States Customs at the border. One method used according to Jose was filling up tires with bundles of drugs and then adding air to them so they would roll and look natural. Another method was the use of a Volkswagon Bug. Apparently the Bug had a compartment which ten kilos (2.2lbs per kilo) of product could be easily concealed. A friend of his had been extremely successful with this method and so Jose adopted it into his operation. The Arkansas trips were time consuming. He would fly out in advance, book a motel, and wait for the shipment of drugs to arrive over land in two Volkswagon Bugs. Jose would then conduct the transaction with his Black connections, and send the money back via the Volkswagon Bugs. His drivers were normally females. He rotated between two groups of females who he called the "Bitches". Two of them were known to be White females and the others were Hispanic. I began to complain to Jose that he was gone a lot, and at times I needed product and he wasn't around. I was actually throwing the blame on to him for my need to have to go elsewhere for product. It was a way to justify purchases of drugs from others in and out of his organization. If someone became suspicious as to why I was purchasing from so many others I had a reasonable argument. I had a lot of targets to choose from and I chose "Fat Ray" to be the next on the hit parade. I had an emphasized special interest in Ray. He thought he was a hardened gangster, and acted like a tough guy. I acquired his telephone numbers, and pager number, and turned them over to the Bureau. I called Ray on one occasion, and got a musical recording in Spanish. A Mexican group singing about organized drug trade, and the Mexican Mafia. I couldn't help but laugh in hysteria. Perhaps it was suppose to be intimidating, or to hoard off evil spirits, but I thought it was hilarious, and I couldn't stop laughing. This guy was a real joke. I disliked him so much that I wanted him to give me a reason so I could pop him up side his head. I think he knew it because he knew where to draw the line with his comments. On another occasion he called and wanted to pick up some MSM after hours. I gave him a hard time over it, and he said, "Hay bitch don't you know I'm a real gangster!" I don't know if I was suppose to be intimidated by the statement, but I laughed, and that pissed him off even more. Perhaps he thought his size was intimidating, who knows what could be in the mind of his great fantasy? "Fat Ray" stood about five feet, eleven inches tall, and weighed about 235 pounds. To someone else he could have looked intimidating, but to me he was a big blob of human shit. I could see clearly right through him. He sometimes came in the store to buy MSM, and always wanted a discount, or wanted to avoid paying the sales tax. I would refuse, and he would get upset. I was tired of him always trying to get over so one day I told him not today, and not any day. As he stood on the customer side of the counter, and I stood behind it with the cash register to my right. I reprimanded him, "You think about who you're talking to, I'm not one of your punk ass friends, I'll jump over this counter, and tear your head off." It was obvious then that I was up set with his running off with the mouth. The expression on face changed, and it appeared as though he was about to shit and piss all over himself. His hands trembled as he handed me the money for the MSM, and left in a hurry. He was well aware of my capabilities after all I had roughed up his boss Paul. Paul and I were on the phone one day and the conversation got heated. The conversation went something like this: I called Paul on my cell phone and as he picked up I said, "Paul this is Tony when are you going to come and see me about that money you owe me?" Paul responded, "Where are you?" My response was, "I'm out and about." Paul came back with a belligerent, "Ya I'm going to see what you're all about!" I took the comment as an insult, and challenge. I felt if I was to maintain credibility, and respect among the others I had to respond swiftly. After Paul made that comment I told him to meet me at my store in ten minutes. I was about to give him his opportunity to find out what I was all about. I arrived at the store first, and had one of my sons with me for back up. A few minutes later Paul arrived with Houseboy Alex and they entered the store. As I let them in I locked the door behind them. Paul stood over in front of the counter and next to a large aquarium stand that was sitting near the counter by the cash register. Alex went over and leaned on one of the shelves to my left rear as I faced Paul. I could clearly see Alex from a rear side view as I was positioned. I closed my right hand into a tight fist and struck him to the chest. The blow drove him back about four feet, and as he traveled in a backward motion he struggled to stay at his feet. I could have continued on but my intent was not to cause injury, but to make a clear, and decisive statement. While Paul struggled to stay on his feet, Alex made a motion to move toward me. When I turned toward him he stopped in his tracks. I stuck out my arm and pointed to him, and I said, "This has nothing to do with you, sit down and have a seat." He didn't take my command serious so I went over and grabbed him by both arms and forcibly sat him down on some bags of crushed corral stacked on the end cap of the gondola. My son had been positioned behind the counter and I yelled over to him, "If he gets up knock him out!" By this time Paul had regained his balance and was in the process of taking off his sun glasses as if he was going to come at me. I advised him, "If you want some of this now is your chance let's go." Paul questioned me with, "What is that all about?" As he stood there all shook up. I got up into his face and told him, "Don't you ever disrespect me, ever. Do you understand?" He then asked, "What did I do?" I then replied, "You f------ told me you wanted to see what I was made of! So if you want to let's go, see what you got!" Then he said, "Look I'm not like that, I'm not into that man, I just want to do my business and that's all." I came back with, "Then don't be talking shit if you're not willing to back it up. Do I look like I'm one of your street buddies where you can get away with your shit talking?" Paul apologized, and asked that I loose his phone numbers because he didn't want to do any more business with me. Paul and Alex left with no further comments. I suppose it was a good thing that my son was there for more reasons than one. First of course for back up, and deter those pea brains from advancing on me. Secondly it would create a sense that my son was hard, willing, and fearless. Not to say that he isn't.

On another occasion "Fat Ray" called me and the conversation went as follows: "Tony it's Ray, I hear your interested in buying some quality stuff? I've got what you want at a better price than your paying guaranteed." I said in return, "Yep, your right I'm in the market for a hook up if the shit is good we continue to do business, if it isn't, it's over. I'll call you and let you know when I'm ready, how's that?" Ray responded, "That's cool call me man, you'll like it, you'll like it, OK call me when you're set." Word was getting around that I was slinging (meaning I was selling drugs), so people on the street thought. What else would I be doing with large quantities of drugs I was purchasing? Little did they know their customer was the Federal Bureau of Investigation. "Fat Ray's" call made my job a whole lot easier because we had gotten past the entrapment issue. Entrapment comes into play as a defense when a defendant claims that he was forced, induced, or encouraged by law enforcement or it's agents to perform an illegal act which he normally would not commit. I went ahead and passed on the information to the powers to be, and they began to work out the details on their end in order to get things rolling. I went ahead and recorded several more conversations with "Fat Ray" and the trap was set. One of those conversations went like this: "Ray I need one big one (one pound) for Tuesday evening." Ray said, "O K I'll call you to make sure on Tuesday morning." I agreed and we waited for Tuesday to arrive. When Ray called Tuesday morning to confirm the deal for the evening I had my recorder set and got everything down. We didn't have a clue as to where the deal would take place so we had to wait it out. According to Ray he worked as grounds keeper at the local Indian Gaming Center. My sources told me he never held a job down in his life, and he was lying.

It was Tuesday 3:30 PM and we had gathered at our rally point on ninth avenue. In the mean time a surveillance team was covering the Indian Gaming Center to follow Ray out. The surveillance team thought they had seen Ray leave. They followed the Ray look-a-like into a Lemoore Tavern. We were receiving calls over the air on this Ray look-a-like when suddenly my cell phone rang. I answered, "Hello who is this?" "It's Ray, I want to do it in the alley behind pioneer apartments," said He. I responded, "That's a negative I'm not going into any secluded alley that I'm not familiar with. Let's do it some where in the open where there are plenty of people where no one will notice anything any body is doing." Ray asked, "O K where?" I said, " The WalMart parking lot towards the Pep Boys side you'll see my truck out there, you won't miss me." It was raining, dark, and a chill in the air. I really enjoyed days like this when I was just a kid. So I felt good about the way things were working out. In the mean time the surveillance team covering the Lemoore Tavern was called off by Kellogg. Kellogg instructed me to stall a little while the video team and back up got into place. Big Bird had been monitoring the air ways for communications between all units involved, and up dating them. I had gone through my rituals of the vehicle check, personal check in order to establish a clear and clean controlled purchase. We counted the money together as always, and I signed for it as "Columbus" as always. Just before departure I was instructed by Kellogg to position my truck so that the surveillance van could video tape the transaction. I was familiar with the van so I knew what to look for. I left the rally point and headed for the WalMart parking lot while taking my time. I drove into the parking lot and looked for the van. I saw it over in the distance and parked kiddy corner, and one lane over, and waited. "Fat Ray" was about to be a movie star, it was a pity it would never hit the big screen." Suddenly I looked over to my right and there was Ray pulling into the open, available space next to me. Ray exited his car, opened my truck door and slid in and shutting the door. Ray took out a plastic bag and handed it to me. I told him, "Take it out of the bag I want to see it." He did so, and I got what I wanted to make sure his finger prints were on the dope wrappings. I was wearing the recording device so getting him on audio tape was an extra bonus. He opened up his side of the conversation with, "Look man I'm a little short so we'll just deduct what I'm short on the money side." I responded upset, "Asshole I told you I needed a full pound man. He was nervous about something and said, "Hay man if anything goes down I'll get the f---- out of hear and head for Mexico." I said in response, "What the hell are you thinking about man!" Inside I was shouting for joy because this would automatically revoke his bail. He had just admitted he would be a flight risk. Later I was told that he was granted bail anyways. It causes me to think that perhaps it was some kind of mistake, or he was cooperating and I was let in on it. After all sometimes it was better I didn't know some of the things that were going on for my own protection. As the money was counted out and he put it into his pocket, and while sliding off the seat and out the door his jacket tightened up and I saw a silhouette of a large frame handgun. This really pissed me off, and had I noticed it earlier I would have taken it from him. I left the WalMart parking lot and headed back to the rally point on Ninth Avenue. Kellogg and Big Bird somehow wound up in front of me, and we arrived at the rally point one behind other. I went through the ritual of the body search, vehicle search, the debriefing, turning in the equipment and a new set of instructions. While recording and still at the rally point I called Ray and told him everything was cool, and I needed another big one on Thursday same time, and same place. Another prosperous day had concluded for me, and I felt good about my work. Thursday came and went with the buy going as planned, and with no unexpected hitches. We now had two confirmed controlled buys on "Fat Ray" and had him clear and clean and not even F. Lee Bailey or Johnny Cochran would get him off.

Jose got back on Friday from his trip and we meet briefly that afternoon just to touch base with him. I told him while he was gone I purchased two pounds from "Fat Ray". I figured it was better he heard it from me than from someone else. It would have gotten back to him by way of Paul. Ray purchased from Paul because Jose didn't like Ray so he wouldn't deal with him. Paul bought from Jose, and Paul found it necessary to bad mouth me every chance he got. On several occasions he tried to convince Jose not to deal with me in any aspect. I knew the information was reliable after all Jose is the one who kept me filled in on Paul's comments. Furthermore, I had become an excellent customer with FBI money, reliable, and always available at his beckoning call with a fresh supply of MSM, so he could cut his Meth down.

CHAPTER FIVE
A WELL DESERVED TIME OUT

IT WAS NOW FEBRUARY 2001 and the work load was taking its toll. I had been working for the Bureau since August, had massed a large quantity of information, and continued working to get closer to Jose and his organization since April 2000. I hadn't taken a vacation in about five years. The stress at home mounted. My family was becoming more convinced I had become an organized crime figure. Perhaps to them I had become some monster that had transformed from a caring, and loving father, and husband into a despicable human being. I felt deeply hurt that they would think of me this way. But on the flip side it was a good thing. If I could convince the people who knew me best of all the real pay off was convincing the bad guys? I felt reassured. I wanted desperately to tell my wife but I knew the way she felt about law enforcement she would have not allowed me to do what needed to be done. Kellogg and Big Bird had offered several times to bring my wife over to the office, and let her in on my work. I felt the time wasn't right and declined.

I thought that a trip to El Paso, Texas to visit our son would help to repair the husband-wife relationship that was being eroded. We spent five days touring the area, and took a drive to Old Whitesands Missile Range to rekindle old memories of almost thirty years before. We experienced different types of dinning each night and over the weekend we went into Juarez, Mexico. We walked across the boarder and had lunch at a restaurant close by the bull fighting arena. We then took a cab to one of the near by market places. We went into every shop with all the shop keepers eager to sell their goods to us. Street peddlers swarming around us trying to induce us to buy something, or even anything they had. It was heart breaking to see them in their worn and torn clothing, but you can't let your feelings over come you after all you can't afford to buy from them all. One old lady was selling peanuts covered in candy, and she really tried her best. I took a moment to look into her aging, and wrinkled face, and I saw a tired old woman trying to survive. I pulled a $20.00 bill placed it into her hand, closed it, and walked away. My thoughts were, I really didn't need that twenty after all I had a bunch more in my pocket just like that one. I looked back, and she had my wife cornered, so my wife bought $5.00 worth of her candy coated peanuts. We went into the shops once again and began to bargain for goods we wanted to take back with us. I wound up buying several colorful wraps, and eight pairs of so called brand named sun glasses. My son, and wife purchased some items, and our day of shopping was completed in Old Mexico. We caught a Taxi cab back to the boarder, got out and paid the driver. There was a long line of people lined up to go through and over to the United States side and the automobile lines were worse. At least the people lines were moving. We went through some detector, questioned by boarder employees and plop we were over in the U.S. of A. side. The first two nights we had stayed at the El Paso Inn on Fort Bliss. My son had a room mate and he was leaving for the weekend. The remainder of the time we stayed with my son at the apartment. The scenery was beautiful at night. From his balcony you could clearly distinguish the border. On the United States side the lighting was more intense, and brighter. The Mexican side was well lit but the lighting was not as intense, a clear distinction. During the day you could see the area of one of the border crossings. A huge Mexican flag flew high into the air and could be seen for many miles. It was truly memorable.

The last night in El Paso was cold and windy, we went out to dinner at a really nice steak house, and out to a large movie theater, and watched the movie "Traffic". How weird to be in a place like El Paso, Texas, doing the work I was doing and watching "Traffic". The following morning my son took us to the airport. We were headed back to the great community of Hanford. I thought the trip would have done us both good, and got me a ticket out of the dog house but it didn't. I went back to work and into the same rut, and back into the dog house I went. If anything I got to see, and spend time with my son, and got the rest I indeed needed. I came back a new and refreshed man ready to take up where I left off. There wouldn't be any controlled buys for a while. The agents were catching up with behind the scene endeavors in support of the intelligence already gathered. They consumed their work hours with surveillance, reports, filing of legal documents, wire taps, and many other things which are required to establish a rock solid case.

CHAPTER SIX
ANXIOUS AND REFRESHED

ALTHOUGH ONLY five controlled purchases had been made up to this point, three of them from Jose and two from Ray there were other deals I was attempting to coordinate, and negotiate under the direction of the Bureau. Jose had been making regular runs to Arkansas approximately every two to three weeks. I was trying to get Jose to allow me to transport a load to Arkansas. I thought I had him convinced to allow me to transport the cocaine to Arkansas on the next trip. The haul would be made in his new black Volkswagon Bug across Interstate 40 straight through to Arkansas. Interstate 40 is known to law enforcement as a drug corridor from California into the Southern, and Eastern states. As I continued to work the idea with Jose the more he seemed to like it. I reported the information back to Kellogg, and Big Bird and the more they liked the idea. We would know the time, date of departure, and control the merchandise in transit. Once I thought the deal had been finalized between Jose and I the Bureau got cold feet. Kellogg explained that Bureau policy dictates that they can not, and will not allow a load of drugs to hit the streets once the drugs came into their control. Going forward with this plan would force the Bureau to take down all the parties involved, and clearly exposing me to all, and bring a premature end to the operation. We had discussed various options, but none of which were favorable to the Bureau. Through my exhausting and convincing efforts it wasn't a total loss. After all I had acquired information giving us vehicle type, estimated time intervals, location, quantities, and type of drivers in control of the vehicle. It included putting Jose at the general area of the transaction. The rest wouldn't be too difficult to piece together. I did as they asked me to do. I told Jose that I was no longer interested in going on the Arkansas run. Being seated for so many hours would make me antsy, and grumpy. Jose felt a little disappointed because after all I was less apt to be pulled over because of age and appearance. Jose added that my age and appearance just didn't fit the typical profile that law enforcement along that corridor looked for as a drug runner. I reinforced my decision not to take on the job, and Jose finally agreed. I thought that since I was successful in gathering so much information on the Arkansas run I would try my luck with his Mexican connection. I began to work Jose, convinced him to take me along on his next Mexican trip. Surprisingly enough he agreed without hesitation. I filled Kellogg, and Big Bird in on what I was doing, and they thought it great for the purpose of gathering information only. Kellogg went on to explain that if I entered Mexico the Mexican Government would have to be notified of my presence, and purpose. The greatest disadvantage was that there would be no cavalry there to back me up if something were to happen. Lastly the Bureau would have to approve it, unless I went across into Mexico totally on my own. I agreed the risk was just too great for me to take, and I decided against it. Nevertheless, Jose's cell phone was being monitored continuously for incoming and outgoing calls.

Jose had mentioned on several occasions that he wanted a means to launder his money and he asked me if I would be interested. We were in my office when the question came up: Jose asked, "What kind of percentage would you charge for converting over money?" I asked, "What do you mean, like laundering money?" Jose responded, "Yep, what would it cost me?" My next question, "Well how much do you want to launder?" Jose was quick to answer, "We can start off small with about a hundred thousand to start." I answered, "Well I'll charge you thirty percent." He seemed to loose interest and we bid our good byes, and he was off on his way. I notified

Kellogg, and briefed him on what had been discussed. He told me he would get back to me on that one. I assumed that his experience in that area was rather limited as was mine, and he probably got some advice on how to handle, and set up a laundering scenario. The following day Kellogg called and instructed me to go ahead and set up the laundering scheme. I called Jose and asked if he was still interested in washing the money. He wasn't interested because thirty percent was just too high. He had someone doing it for five percent. I responded with an offer of three percent, and he jumped on it. He agreed and wanted to met with me the following Thursday and pick up seventy thousand. I told him it would take five to seven days before he got his money back cleaned from a friend of mine from Los Angeles who was an accountant.

Thursday arrived I had gone through a briefing with Kellogg and Big Bird at a new rally point I had selected. Surveillance was set up, and I had my recording device on and ready to go. I called Jose to confirm everything was a go. Jose picked up and said, "Tony Montana what are you doing?" I responded with, "I'm on my way over to see to take care of that business we talked about." Jose pleasantly answered, "O K I'm here waiting come on over." I departed with Kellogg's vehicle a short distance behind me. As I drove up to a cross street before Galileo Street where Jose lived he was out there standing and looking down the street all hyped up. It was clear he was pumped up about something. I pulled onto Galileo, and parked just short of being in front of his house. He came up to me as I was exiting my truck. I thought for sure he had noticed Kellogg and Big Bird drive by just behind me, but he made no mention. Perhaps with all his excitement he hadn't become suspicious of them. He began saying, "Ya we were getting a load ready to send out and I happened to look out the window and I saw these "Sons of Bitches" looking at all the cars and writing shit down. I came running out of the house right on up to them and I saw their jackets it said "Special Rural Unit". They were cops. So I started yelling hay what you want so they backed up in a hurry and zipped out of here." I told him, "Its' O K they're gone don't worry about it they were probably just harassing you, messing with your head. Let's go ahead and take care of that business." Jose upset answered, "No I don't want to do it now, the hell with it, I got this shit to worry about now. My car drove off I hope it made it." Just then his cell phone rang. "Jose answered, "Ya did you make it alright? Is everything cool? Good, good, O K later then if anything happens call me back." Jose had affirmed that he didn't want to launder the money, and I left and made my way back to the rally point. As I left I called Kellogg on the cell and told him to meet me at our spot. I was upset with the Sheriff's Office because that was their unit. It was a special unit out of the Sheriff's Office that works agricultural crimes. What the hell were they doing harassing Jose? Local law enforcement was supposed to have been told hands off on Jose, and his band of merry men. I briefed Kellogg, and Big Bird, and they began to make up off the wall excuses. I looked at it as a screw up, some stupid local boys up to their bull crap as usual. After that fiasco Kellogg continued to encourage me to set up another laundry transaction. I refused, and told him to have his agriculture unit do it for him. I was up set and wasn't going to waste any more of my time just to have them mess it all up. I wasn't up for playing games, they screwed it up, and they had to live with it. I later thought perhaps the screw up was intended. Jose would get back a check. After deposited it could lead the Bureau to hidden money. Perhaps someone didn't want that to happen?

A few more days had passed since getting back from El Paso. I was in my office and my cell rang. It was Jesse, "Tony I need to come over and see you, we need to talk its' important." I answered, "O K come right over I'm waiting." Twenty minutes hadn't passed and Jesse arrived along with Alex. Alex happened to be Jesse's right hand man more of an errand boy than anything. We went over to my dirt road just west of the house where we were secluded from everyone. Jesse began to explain the reason for the meeting, "Jose is out of town and ran into some difficulties while down in Mexico. He lost a load of cocaine, eleven kilos to be exact. The two bitch drivers were caught at the border with the shit trying to come over. They're talking and he's got some serious problems. I wanted to be able to sell you stuff, and I'll sell it cheaper that Jose has been selling to you, and better quality. What do you say, for the Meth $2,600.00 a pound, how's that?" I replied, "Well if your product is of the same quality or better, and cheaper priced then I don't see why we can't do business. After all Jose is gone a lot, and sometimes he isn't around when I need product so it won't hurt to have you as back up. I'm good right now, I won't need anything for a week or so, I'll call you and let you know for sure how much, and when." Jesse was happy and responded, "O K I'll wait for your call but we have got a deal, right?" I agreed with, "Yep I'll call you at least a day before to give you a heads up." The logic in it all was that Jose's risk factor had just increased significantly. In reality Jose was a wounded animal, and the others smelled blood, and they were coming in for the kill. Jesse had gone around to Jose's customers and tried to convince them to make a switch. What Jesse was really trying to do is take over. Jesse figured that Jose was at his most vulnerable state because this was his third large loss in a short time. Jose had sent a shipment of drugs to Kentucky. Law enforcement had intercepted the two drivers on the way back. They found $170,000.00 in cash with cocaine residue on it. Authorities seized the vehicle, found the money and took them into custody. In the mean time Jose attempted to transport a shipment of cocaine through Mexico on a bus. The bus was pulled over, search by the Federales and the cocaine was found, and confiscated. The loss estimated to be approximately at $400,000.00. These significant losses caused Jose to panic, and become extremely stressed. After all he had just lost a small fortune, and was probably indebted to someone for several hundred thousands of dollars, enough to have stressed out anyone.

The same day I met with Jesse and shortly after the meeting, Jose called me from Delta View Hospital Emergency Room in Visalia, from his cell phone. He was being treated for a stab wound to the left side of his abdomen. He wanted to meet with me at his place on Evergreen in about an hour. An hour ticked on by and I was at his house on Evergreen. I exited my truck, made my way up the walk way, rang the door bell, and the door opened almost immediately. It seemed as if he had been waiting right there by the door. Jose said loudly, "Tony Montana." I walked through the doorway, and he closed it behind me. He stepped over toward me, and hugged me. It caught me by surprise, because he had never displayed this type of friendship before. Nevertheless, I played along and hugged him back. As he withdrew from the hug I looked into his eyes, and caught him looking, and searching deep into mine. I saw a face like I had not seen before. He looked tired as though he hadn't had a restful night in a while, and he was showing signs of stress. He wasn't himself. He lifted his shirt, and showed me a fresh wound at the side of his abdomen about and inch long, but no telling how deep it went. He invited me into the kitchen, and asked me to sit down. Jose began to share with me about all of his bad luck. As he went through and told me of his great misfortunes he sat directly across from me at the kitchen table, and looking directly into my eyes, as if to be searching for something. He told me about the incident at the San Diego border. He had lost the new Black Volkswagon Bug he had just purchased two months before. The two female drivers were talking, and he was worried. In addition the loss of the $170,000.00 while returning from Kentucky after the sale of a load of cocaine. No telling about the drivers, whether they were cooperating with authorities or not. Then the cocaine shipment lost in Guadalajara. As he told me about all the mishaps he continued to try, and pierce through my eyes, and I guess try and look into my soul. Then he went on to tell me that Jesse had been making the rounds to his clientele in an attempt to win them over. Jose was extremely upset, and threatened to kill Jesse. He had already put the word out that he wanted Jesse dead, and it was going to happen soon. I told Jose that Jesse had been over to see me and offered me Meth at $2,400.00 a pound. I went on to tell Jose, "Jose you and I have done a lot of business together and I would rather do it with you than with him, but when you're not around I have to get my supply from someone." This was my excuse for going around and purchasing drugs from the others. I didn't want them getting suspicious as why I was buying from so many of them. I refocused the conversation back to Jesse. I told Jose that killing Jesse was a real bad business move. If killing erupted then the authorities would become a lot more pro active, and it would bring a lot of unnecessary heat down upon us and interrupt our lucrative drug enterprise. It would make things very difficult to operate as comfortably as we did, and only adding to our problems. The way to take care of Jesse would be through wise business decisions, and put him out of business without the use of violence. He seemed to still be convinced in taking Jesse out. In the meantime Jose wanted a commitment from me that I wouldn't sell anymore MSM to anyone, especially Jesse. He wanted to control the MSM. As an incentive, Jose would purchase all the MSM I had on the shelf, and anything I had incoming to include a standing order of one hundred pounds a month. I agreed to the offer, and we shook hands on it. The next question which came from his lips took me to an all time level of concern. Jose asked, "Do you know where Officer Hoover with the Hanford P.D. lives?" I must have had a surprised look on my face, and responded, "No I don't why do you want to know where he lives?" Jose blurted back, "Because I want to take him out too. Can you find out where he lives?" I told Jose, "I've never seen him, I don't know what he looks like, and I don't know how I would find out, but I could try and throw some lines out, and see what I can come up with. Still this isn't a very good idea killing a cop. You know how much heat that would bring. Not only would you have the locals looking till hell freezes over, but the state cops would come in, and that isn't the least of it. The Feds of all people would be in here rolling over every stone, and rock. They wouldn't stop until they had someone hooked-up. Shit man you better really think that one over." I concluded the conversation with, "Look, I'll come by tomorrow, and we'll talk some more, and may be you'll be feeling better." He agreed and I left. I waited until I was down the street a ways and dialed Kellogg on the cell phone. I briefed Kellogg in on what had taken place. Kellogg was concerned about Jessie's safety and asked me if I thought Jose was really serious about going through with the hit on Jessie. I responded in the affirmative. Kellogg was concerned with assigning personnel to cover, and watch Jessie for his protection, or just take him into protective custody for his own safety. Kellogg decided to have Jessie covered with the assigning of a surveillance team. This was the only logical measure he could take in order to preserve the integrity of the operation. Otherwise, if they plucked Jessie off the street they would have had to close down the operation prematurely, and a lot of Jose's people would slip through the cracks, and continue with their dealings. Kellogg congratulated me for a job well done for trying to talk Jose out of carry out the hits.

The next day I went over to see Jose at about ten A.M. He came to the door, and let me in. I had awoken him from his sleep, and he still looked worn, and stressed out. We went into the living room, and sat down on the huge, black, leather sectional sofa with a huge, big screen television directly out in front of us. We began to discuss the situation with Jessie. Jose had thought about what I had said the night before about placing Jessie out of business instead of resorting to violence, and agreed that I was right. I congratulated him on a wise choice, and an excellent business move. Nevertheless, I expressed my feelings about Jessie; he was a no good son of a bitch, and deserved to get popped, and I really didn't give a shit one way or the other. After all I didn't want Jose to think I was getting soft, or that I had a special place in my heart for Jessie. Again I congratulated Jose on a wise business move, and comforted him by telling him that all this was a mild set back, and the cost of doing business. I stressed that perhaps it might be a good time for Jose to get out of business altogether, and legitimize to an honest way of making a living. After all by now he must have a nice little nest egg put a side. Jose almost immediately declined saying that he needed at least another year before he could step down. In my thoughts all I could think about at that moment was all the lives that would be affected during that one more year he needed. As far as I was concerned that wasn't going to happen.

I was pleased with myself for talking Jose out of killing Jessie, and Hoover. There was no way to foresee how many other people could have gotten hurt in the process. After all it was the ethical and moral thing to do. Jesse deserved death for all the destruction he was responsible for, but it was up to the courts. In Jesse's days of slinging dope, how much dope was he responsible for placing onto the streets of our community? How many overdoses was he responsible for? How many crack babies did his drugs create? How many parents became dependant, and caused their children to be deprived of their basic needs? There were just too many children going to bed hungry simply because their cub bards were bare. All because Jesse, and the others had a material greedy appetite they felt they had to feed at the extremely painful expense of many innocent children.

I arranged a controlled purchase with Jesse which was supposed to take place at his residence. He backed out wanting to do the deal at his house, and continued to delay the deal beyond the agreed time. Finally, Jesse had backed out of doing the deal himself, and arranged Alex to carry out the transaction. I suppose Jesse thought he was creating some type of safety buffer between him and the sale of the drugs. He was mistaken after all the deal had been recorded, and he was being watched. In the very least there would be a solid charge of conspiracy and solicitation; since he had approached me in an offer to sell me meth. It didn't matter who was going to do the deal after all we were about to get two for the price of one. Finally, I got a telephone call on the cell from Alex. I told him to meet me at the Walmart parking lot in front of the Pep Boys Auto Parts Store. It was the same place where we had done the buys with Ray. Alex was apprehensive, and wanted to stall some more for what ever reason I'll never know. I got firm with him and told him it was either now, or never. No business today, meant no business ever. What was it going to be? He agreed to stop with the delays and to let us get the deal over with. Kellogg was sitting in my truck while the conversation was recorded, and he gave Big Bird the signal to get the teams into place, it was a go. Kellogg gave me my final last minute instructions, and waited a few minutes in order to allow the teams ample time. After about ten minutes I began to roll, and Alex called over the cell letting me know he was held up at the train tracks. I called Kellogg and gave him a heads up on the call. As I parked into a comfortable spot the cell rang. It was Kevin giving me a heads up that Alex was in the parking lot and headed towards me. A few moments later Alex rolled up in his Dodge Intrepid, and parked along side of me. He exited his car, went to the trunk, opened it up, and pulled out a black plastic bag. He walked over to me, and hopped into the passenger side seat of my truck. He handed me the bag. I sensed he was very nervous. I opened up the bag, and looked inside. It looked like the real stuff. I smelled it, and it smelled like the real stuff. I counted out the money while he assured me it was good product, and that I would be satisfied still showing signs of nervousness. He placed the money into his pocket, exited the truck for his car, and left the parking lot. In the mean time I headed for our new rally point while they had a team follow Alex right back to Jessie with the money. I arrived at our new rally point with Kellogg, and Big Bird right behind. Content with the out come my cell phone rang. Big Bird yelling through the phone, "Tony, we have an unknown on our tail take evasive measures we don't know who he is!" I felt the hairs on my neck stand up, and I pulled a radical U-turn and headed out the entrance. Our rally point only had one way in, and the same way out. I zipped right past the mystery vehicle, and out the entrance, at the same time looking through my rear view mirror. After all I didn't want to breach the integrity of the controlled buy by not being in their sight at all times. I noticed that Big Bird was pulled along side the mystery vehicle, and talking to him. Another call came over the cell. It was Big Bird telling me that the unknown was one of theirs. I turned my vehicle around, and met with them at the rear where we were well concealed from the road.

We all got out of our vehicles introductions were made while my heart was still pounding, and nearly exiting my chest. It was one of the guys from the State Narcotics Bureau. He was there to take possession of the drugs. I was debriefed and went through the normal of calling it a day of playing around with your local drug dealer. I went home, and tried to unwind over an ice cold Pepsi Cola.

CHAPTER SEVEN
Coming Down The Home Stretch

We were coming into the end of March and we were gearing up for another controlled buy. This one was for Israel, Jose's younger brother. Israel had been calling me on a regular basis, and trying to persuade me to buy from him. Word was getting around town about all the drugs I had been purchasing. Many different ballers approached me trying to get me to buy from them. Many of them I turned away because they were small peanuts. They were users trying to make it higher up on the food chain. Some of the times I would laugh at them, and tell them may be I'll sell you some, and then quote them a ridiculous low price. Then they would offer to buy from me, and I would respond with, "you can't buy enough for me to be bothered." I would toy with them until to no avail they gave up the conversation. After all the mission wasn't focused on the street level dealers it was the top dogs we wanted to take out.

I liked Israel a lot because he was just a young stupid kid who was brought up in this environment. It was acceptable within his family, and that is what he knew. After all he had been conditioned to think that way. I often thought about the day I would have to do the buy from him. I thought about the hard time he would have to do for his deeds. He was eighteen years old, and awfully young to fall hard, and do some serious time. I remember sitting on my truck tailgate, at two in the morning looking up into the sky, and bright stars. I would think about all those innocent people's lives ruined by the drugs he placed into the community. I tried to be objective, and look at things from both views. I wanted to search my soul to try and better understand why he dealt drugs, and search for reasons to justify it for him. In my deep search I couldn't find any reason. Again the thought of all those people who became victims of his drugs reinforced the reasons for doing what I had to continue to do. Local law enforcement in this community had been working the drug scene forever, and they had never succeeded on making an impact of any significance. The locals didn't have the leadership, or desire to put the big boys out of business. They continued to operate the conventional way, lacked sophistication, and the overall street smarts that it takes to get the job done. Therefore, I guess I was the only thing standing between the big boys, and innocence. At least that is how I felt for the moment.

I remember receiving a call from Israel wanting to come over, and pick up some MSM. I thought I would toy with him a bit, and create some conversation among him, and Jose. I had a scale that we had used in the Feed Store, and took it out and placed it on the table in my office. I quickly took some MSM and melted it, placed it out in plain view onto the scale, and waited for Israel to arrive. I let Israel in the office and he was surprised to see what appeared to be Meth on the scale. I told him it was new product that had just come in. He didn't look too happy about it. He purchased the bucket of MSM, and left. I wanted it to appear that I was doing more than they thought I was, and perhaps help move things along. It would also play as a convincing piece, and cause discussion among them. The next day Kellogg, Big Bird, and I all meet down at the rally point. Overland Stockyards had become my rally point of choice. After all the rear area was secluded and I felt comfortable. We all waited around for some time. I went through the normal ritual, got equipped, thoroughly searched, and briefed. I signed for the money, and made the call while recording it. I got on the cell phone, and called Israel. Israel picked up and said, "Tony Montana, I'll have everything ready in about thirty minutes." I then replied, "Hay, I don't have all day you better get your shit together." "Yep thirty minutes guaranteed," he replied back. Israel had lowered his price to $2,500.00 a pound in order to compete with Jessie. I waited thirty minutes, and called him back, and told him that his time was up. I was coming over to pick it up at his residence at Galileo Street. I headed over with Kellogg and Big Bird close behind. The surveillance team was already in place, and a bird was in the air. Israel was outside playing basketball when I pulled up, parked, got out of my pickup, we shook hands, and went in the house. We went into Israel's bedroom, and sat down. There was a noise of a vehicle pulling up outside. Israel looked out the bedroom window, and told me to hold up. He went outside, and came right back in with product wrapped in a towel. I looked at it, and could smell it although it was tightly wrapped. I placed it into a plastic bag, and counted out the money. Each time I counted it I came up $100.00 short. I knew the money was all there because Kellogg and I had both counted it together when I signed for it back at the rally point. I knew my count was defective. The money must have been sticking together. I finally got frustrated, and just handed all the money to him, and told him I knew it was all there. Nevertheless, I got it all down on tape. I left the house with the goods, and headed back to the rally point. After I had arrived with Kellogg, and Big Bird present a long time familiar Bureau of Narcotics Enforcement Agent pulled up right behind us. I was glad to see a familiar face after the previous experience last time. It was Fred and I hadn't seen him in months. Fred got out of his car just raving with laughter, and a smile stretched from ear to ear. You would have thought that he was the one to make the buy. He said walking toward me, "Tony, your batting a hundred percent aren't you? When you get done working for these guys you need to come and work for us. You have an incredible and unheard of record, wow!" He went on raving about me. I cracked a huge smile of my own and said, "Yep I'm bad, I'm bad!" I looked over at Big Bird and Kellogg and it seemed that perhaps they didn't like something that Fred had said. They probably didn't care to much for the comment, "You can come work for us once your done with these guys." This controlled buy had just reeled in

Israel. As I was in the house waiting for Israel to return from outside Furbee had driven up and handed Israel the goods, and drove off. This buy now implicated Furbee and brought him into the realm of a conspiracy charge, possession for sales, and transportation. Again we had just got two for the price of one. They were racking up, and at the same time Big Bird, Kellogg, and the surveillance team continued on with their work of tracking, locating, and collecting evidence to establish a rock solid case against these hoodlums.

We entered into April, and the FBI was busy doing all the things, behind-the-scenes they normally do. I continued to supply Jose with large quantities of MSM with the approval, and under the supervision of the FBI.

Sometime during the first week of April I met with Jose, and discussed the possibility of purchasing large quantities of cocaine to be shipped into Boston, and possibly Miami. I told them I would first purchase a sample, and have it transported back into Boston aboard a big rig. I told him I had a relative in Boston who had a few big rigs. His drivers drove into Las Vegas weekly with loads of food products for the casinos. On the way back they came into California to pick up goods to haul back to the east coast. Before heading back I would hook up with them, and give them the dope to take back. The story was convincing, and he bought it. I didn't feed him this story all at once. I had built up to it a little at a time on occasions when we would met I'd mention something about my relative with the trucks. I went ahead and gave him the order for the sample: I told him, "Look Jose I need probably half a pound as a trial sample. If the shit is good then we'll go from there. How much will you charge me for the half?" Jose replied anxiously, "I sell a pound for sixteen thousand dollars so half of that, eight thousand." I then said, "That's good, I'll call you and we'll set it up for later on in the week. How much notice will you need?" Jose concluded with, "What ever you need there is plenty on the shelf."

I phoned Kellogg, and told him I needed eight thousand dollars for the buy. Kellogg assured me that wouldn't be a problem. I called Jose on Saturday, April 7th and told him it was a go for Sunday, the following day. Jose assured me it would be ready.

Sunday arrived I had gotten a good nights sleep, and felt like it would be a great day. Things began to go wrong: Kellogg called and said there would be a delay. My wife was upset because I told her I was busy, and didn't have time to spend with her, and the family. She was not happy, and I couldn't blame her because this was one of many Sundays I had dedicated to someone else. She began to think that I was having an affair so our relationship at times became extremely heated. I was in the house waiting when I received a call from Big Bird, and I went outside to take the call on the cell phone. Yet another delay as Big Bird went on to explain. He probably assumed that I was upset with them but I wasn't in the least. I understood that sometimes things go wrong, and there are delays. He finally opened up, and told me there was a problem with the airplane they needed to fix a part. I told him I knew how it was with aircraft. After all I worked on aircraft while in the Marine Corps. I responded with let me know when your ready to roll. Forty-five minutes later the call I had been waiting for. It was Big Bird we were ready to rumble. The aircraft was repaired, and ready to get into the air. We met at the rally point at the Stockyards in the rear. I called Jose, told him I was ready my people were in town, but not to make it an all day thing. The surveillance team was in place, and the aircraft was on stand by at the airport. Communication came over the radio that Furbee and Jose were on the move, and the phone lines were hot. They were driving crazy in their own style in an effort to avoid being followed. Jose called, and said he didn't want to do it at his place as originally planned, so I suggested we do it at my place out in front of the store. Jose said he would call me back. We continued to wait at the stockyard, and monitored the radio transmissions. We went through our rituals of searching, briefing, preparing the recording device I wore, and recorded all incoming calls. Suddenly my cell phone rang again. I thought it was Jose, but when I looked at the screen it was Israel's number that appeared. I answered, "Hello who is this?" Israel responded with, "Hay I wanted to know how you liked that other stuff, it was good uh?" I snapped back with, "Israel, I'm really busy right now, I'm in the middle of some shit right now, and I'll get back to you when I get a chance." Then I hung up. It caught me off guard, I couldn't think of any reason why he would call at such a time. The timing bothered me. After giving it some thought I concluded that Israel was probably aware that I was buying eight-thousand dollars worth from Jose, and he was pissed-off, and couldn't understand why I didn't buy it from him. He was probably upset because that was eight-thousand dollars that he wouldn't get a cut from. A while later Jose called, "Hay Montana I'm ready I'll met you at your place in five minutes. We had to buy a little time to get people in place so I waited a few minutes before I left. I was instructed not to go inside the store, and keep the transaction outside. My instinct and experience had already made me aware of exactly that. A couple of vehicles left before I did to get into position. I strapped on my recorder, and off I went. About half a mile from my place I received a call. I checked my screen, and it was Jose again. I answered, "Hello, what?" "Where are you man? I'm here waiting at your place?" Jose snapped back. Reassuring Jose I replied, "Hay I'm just a minute away, down the street, I'll be right there!" As I pulled in Jose was parked next to my son's pickup truck at an angle. He was sitting in the passenger side, and Stud Muffin was in the driver's seat. I pulled in right behind them, and we all exited at once. Jose came over, and shook my hand as he always did. We began to small talk and joked as we always did. Jose seemed really nervous, and continued to look around, and over his shoulder. I noticed that he was looking me over from head to toe. He looked right at my beeper recording device as it hung outside my pants, and shirt. I thought I was going to have a problem, but he just continued to stare right at it. I then turned so that it was out of his sight, and asked where the hell is the shit in an effort to get anything he might have seemed suspicious of out of his mind. He knew that I normally didn't carry a beeper, and he didn't have access to that number, so it could have become an issue. I felt I was lucky. I was successful in distracting him because he looked up at me, and said it will be right here. He got on his cell phone and called someone, "Where are you?" he asked. "O. K.," he said into the phone. Right after he got off the phone Furbee arrived. He got out of the black Chevy Barreta he was driving, and handed me the cocaine in a clear plastic zip lock bag. It was like I said earlier this guy really didn't have any smarts. I immediately covered it up as if I were really concerned. I yelled at him, "You dumb shit are you stupid, or what right out in the open what brains!" I looked at the stuff. It was off white, and looked to be Meth. I got upset and thought they had brought me the wrong stuff. I said, "Shit this is the wrong shit man!" They began to laugh, "No that's the right shit!" I took a whiff and realized it was cocaine. It wasn't what I had seen the first time. The cocaine really smelled strong. Jose and I got into my truck, and I passed him the eight thousand dollars. We began to discuss the cocaine that was in the bag. He showed me the brand marking left from the mold. I later learned that the cocaine cartels use molds with distinguishing markings, or logos that imprint into the cocaine. From these mold imprints they are able to identify which cartel the cocaine came from. It was a great piece of information that could be used at a later date. We bid our good bys, and parted our separate ways. I headed back to our rally point, and Jose took off in the opposite direction, and eventually headed east down highway 198 towards Visalia. I pulled into the stockyards, and parked. Kellogg and Big Bird pulled in directly behind me, and Fred following right behind them. We went through our normal routine of searching, taking in the evidence, the debriefing, and the signing for the money spent. Fred had exited his car with again a huge smile on his face commenting as he walked over towards me, "This puts you at eight for nine?" I quickly responded, no it's eight for eight! Are you trying to lower my percentages?" He replied, I've never heard of such success in all my years!" I bid my good bye, and collected my pat on the back and "good job" and headed for home. As I pulled in I attempted to immediately unwind, but it was difficult. My mind was traveling a thousand miles per minute, and the adrenaline was still in high. I went over to my Pepsi Machine in front of my store, and bought a well deserved cold one. I walked over to the pickup turned on the stereo, and sat on my tailgate. I sat there swinging my legs back, and forth, sipping on the Pepsi, and thinking about the impact that the day's activity would soon have upon the lives of these bad people. I still had a problem I soon had to face, and it didn't have anything to do with drug dealers. My wife would soon be home, and no telling how she was going to react for not spending the day with her. She got home later that evening, and started right in on me with first her silent treatment. Then she off loaded on me going on about spending all this time with these low lives, and probably doing bad things with them. My wife, the love of my life of who I had shared many things with over twenty-six years of marriage. She was caring, kind, and loving. She is a great mother and wife. I couldn't bear keeping the secret from her any longer it had to come out. I was hurting inside, and I could see she was distressed over what seemed to be going on. That evening in the bedroom, with the door closed I told her I was working for the FBI. My mission was to take the drug dealers out. I couldn't tell her any more but I would arrange for her to meet with Kellogg, and Big Bird. If the occasion called for it they could go into further detail. When I finally came out with the truth I couldn't read her facial expression. Nevertheless, she expressed relief that I wasn't doing things to violate the law. I must have stretched my secret out to the limit with my family because she told me that night she was going to pack up, and leave with the kids. I was relieved, and slept very well that night. The next morning the conversation picked up where it left off, but it was brief. She and I were both preparing for work, and time was of the essence. The moment of truth was about to come upon me. The bad thoughts and beliefs my children had about me were about to be exchanged for the truth. My son Jarod had been told months before, but nothing was discussed in depth. He was someone I came to trust with my secret because he was too close, and around me all the time. He began to piece things together while walking in, or over hearing conversations going on over the telephone. Once he walked into my office while I was recording one of the conversations with Jose. Things were becoming obvious to him, and there was no way around it. It just became the nature of the beast that had to dealt with.

One day I went over to pick up my youngest son from school. It wasn't a common practice for me to pick him up, and he was surprised to see me. He jumped into the truck with his backpack and we made our way through the congestion around the school. I asked him if he was hungry, and he responded no. I really thought he would of said yes. Any kid his age is normally always hungry. I was flabbergasted with the no. I responded with yes you are so we're going to get a bite. He looked at me rather funny, crinkled up his forehead, lowering his eye brows, and said O.K. We arrived at the local Arby's, ordered our food, and took a seat. I began with, "Caleb I have something really important to tell you, but before I tell you, you must promise you will tell no one, and you will keep it a secret." With a strange look on his face, "Yes dad I promise." Hesitating with difficulty only because I didn't know how he would handle it I said, "I'm working for the FBI to take all these drug dealers off the street." The expression on his face changed with exclamation and he said, "Wow that's cool my dad is working for the FBI! I'm proud of you dad and relived that your doing something good." I was later told that he had been worried about me, and about the bad company I was keeping. That was probably the cause for the misbehaving he was doing in school. Things that trouble children affect them in different ways, and this is how it affected him. I felt really guilty that I was the cause of creating just another issue in his life he had to deal with. After all life it is tough enough for children as it is, let alone contributing to the load already upon them. I hoped that he would understand, and forgive me. I chose to tell my son Adam next. Sources had informed me that he had become disgusted with me. I called him, and asked him to come down from Fresno to see me as soon as it was convenient. He came down that same day. He came in, and we sat down in the living room. I began with, "Adam do you know all those drug dealers I've been in association with, well there is a very good reason for it. I'm working for the FBI and we're working on taking them all off the streets." He responded with, "Dad don't be fooling around like that, you always want to joke around!" In reply I said, "It's the truth I'm not playing." After a few minutes of intense convincing he finally believed me. He began to ask a whole lot of questions as I knew he would, because that's Adam. I told him we could not discuss it any further, he had to keep it quiet, tell no one, and it will all be over soon.

My most difficult hurdle was yet to come. I still had my daughter to break the news to. I gave it a lot of thought, and struggled with it. I wanted to break it to her gently, but I didn't know what gentle was in this case. I called her on the phone, and asked her to come over if she wasn't busy because I had something to share with her. My wife got on the phone and told her it was really important. She didn't waste any time and came right over. We sat down in the living room and by the expression on her face I could tell she was expecting the worst. She looked as though she was ready to break down and cry. As I finished breaking the news to her she asked, "You and mom aren't breaking up?" I responded with a flat, "No!" She went on with, "And no one has a terminal disease or anything?" Again I responded with, "No!" Her facial expression changed from distress to relief. I began to laugh only to break the tension in the room. It was so thick you would have to use a power saw to cut through it.

A few days later I told Kellogg and Big Bird and filled everyone in, and explained how the necessity had developed. They were glad that my wife was receptive, and supportive as she was.

A few days had passed and I received a call from Jose. He wanted to know what my sources in Boston had thought of the $8,000.00 worth of cocaine. I told him the situation looked favorable, but it was still going to take at least a few more days before a decision was made. I called Kellogg, and he wanted me to continue to stall which I did. I didn't ask any questions I just did it. I knew that what ever the hold up was that there was a good reason behind it.

The FBI was taking a long time to get their shit together so I told Kellogg I was going over to see Jose, and at least begin negotiations to keep him on the hook, and interested. I didn't want Jose to think I was blowing smoke. I placed the call, and asked him when it would be a good time to come over and discuss business. He told me to come right over. I drove over to Evergreen where he lived, and where he would be waiting for me. I pulled into the driveway and parked right in front of his garage. I got out, walked over to the door, and as I was about to ring the door bell when he opened the door. We exchanged greetings as I entered, and he closed the door behind us. We went over and sat at the kitchen table. I opened up the conversation with, "I don't know how much you can handle so I don't know where to begin." Jose replied, "I'm going to need more cocaine. I'm getting low, and I usually buy twenty kilos of coke at a time. If you match it with a purchase of an additional twenty keys I can reduce the price to you $1,500.00 per key. In fact I will do better, and will bring your purchase price down to $14,300.00 per key. That is a thirty thousand dollar savings to you." I found the offer to be attractive and replied, "I don't know if my people can handle twenty keys at a wack." That's a lot of cash, but if I kick in about seventy thousand of my own money I think we could swing it." Jose responded with, "I'll even take you over to meet my boss, and the next time you need cocaine you can go, and negotiate the deal yourself, and he'll give me my cut later." In surprise but suspicious I replied, "That' really great that you're willing to introduce me to him, but I'm not sure if I want to do business with anyone other than you. I know you, I don't know this guy." Jose came back with, "It's cool. This guy is my uncle. Nothing is going to happen to you." In caution I said, "You know what Jose? People kill people for a lot less than $286,000.00 every day." Jose replied with, "Yep that's true." I responded with, "Look I'll get back to you. Give me a day or two to work things out." We said our good byes as usual. A block away from Jose's Evergreen residence I got on the cell phone, and called Kellogg. I opened the conversation with, "Hay Corn Flake Man I got a surprise for you, Jose wants to take me in to meet his uncle, the big cocaine man himself. He wants to sell me twenty kilos." With a surprised tone in Kellogg's voice he replied, "That's great! I give you eight-thousand for a simple coke buy, and you turn it into a half a million dollar deal! That's great let me get to work on it and I'll see what I can do on this end." Curiously I asked, "You think there might be any trouble getting this money at least for flashing?" Kellogg quickly responded with excitement in is voice, "No there won't be any problem. Stall and don't consummate any deal. Give me time to get things on my end together." It was clear that Kellogg was excited. As for me there aren't words that could express how excited I felt. I knew that after this case was over I would be burnt, and would probably never work undercover in this area again. If that was the case I wanted my exposure to be maximized, and make it a gigantic pay off.

Friction began to increase between Kellogg and myself over the availability of the money for the large cocaine buy. Kellogg kept changing the rules, and could never seem to come together. First we discussed me going in with the money, and it would result in a buy-bust. Then we discussed producing the money just to flash, just to show Jose that I really had the money, and I was for real. One of the agents, would pull up in a vehicle open up a brief case, and let Jose see the money, and then speed away with the cash. Then the scenario changed again. There was never going to really be any money. All this "bull" was making me uncomfortable. First, I couldn't believe they couldn't come up with that kind of money. Secondly, and more likely no one had the "balls" to sign out for that kind of money, and place it at risk with some possibility that perhaps it could be lost. What Kellogg and I did agree on was that I would go ahead and call Jose and discuss the arrangements for the purchase. I called Jose, "We're ready to roll but instead of twenty kilos I want to up it to twenty-five kilos. Can you handle that?" Jose replied with, "I can handle it no problem." I went on with, "Let's do it for Monday, April 30." Jose agreed with, "That's fine. I'll tell you what, since you don't want to meet my uncle I'll pick it up early so you can look at it. I'll let you look at it on Sunday, the day before." I responded with approval and the deal was on.

Sunday, April 30 came and things were hopping. The surveillance teams were in place and Kellogg and I were at the rally point waiting to hear from Jose. I finally called him, and he said he was working on it , and he would call as soon as things were ready. We continued to wait, and to no avail the viewing of the cocaine never materialized. I finally called Jose back because it was getting late. He told me he would have it for me on Monday, and he swore on his dead baby's soul. What ever that was suppose to mean I told him fine and we called it a day. I was never told but I realized that Jose had been placed on twenty-four hour surveillance, and things were not about to change. Each time we had an arrangement with Jose the surveillance teams were on him. While Kellogg, Big Bird, and I waited for our cue we continued to listen to communications coming over the radios. It was clearly evident that the teams were close by and watching and watching our boy's every move. Monday had arrived and we had repeated Sunday's script. We meet at the rally point, with everyone in place, and we waited. I placed a call into Jose after I was briefed, and we went through our rituals. Jose had backed out once again. Jose wanted to set it up for Tuesday, at 10 P.M. Nevertheless, Jose promised that the cocaine would be there at the Evergreen residence by 10 P.M. I told him my people were not going to hang around town waiting for the shit, so it better be there. He reassured me that it would. Tuesday morning Jose called, and said that everything was a go on his end. The stuff would be there at eight. I told him it would take place at ten because I wanted my people leaving town with the shit with the advantage of the cover of darkness. He said he understood, but there was a slight change. He had to have $15,500.00 for each Kilo. I got my cal-

culator out, and figured it was another $30,000.00. I told him
I didn't think we could afford the twenty-five kilos. We would
go twenty kilos instead. The whole time the conversation was
being recorded. He sounded a little disappointed, but agreed.
We hung up, and I waited a few minutes to call him back. I
wanted him to gather the impression that perhaps I was checking it out with someone on the other end. I got ready again and
made the call. I told him we would take the twenty-five keys
after all, even at the new price, but now we can't do the deal
until Wednesday at twelve noon. He immediately got upset,
and began to repeat F----, F----, many times on the phone. I
reminded him that he was the one who made the last minute
changes to the agreement, and threw everything off track, and
not me. Therefore, I explained to him that I needed extra time
to round up that much more money. Then he offered to credit
me the extra thirty-five thousand. I could pay it later so as not
to throw off the schedule we had already planned out. I told
him I didn't like owing him that kind of money, and I wanted
to pay it all at once. Besides, it was beautiful with his greed he
just feel into the plan completely. As if it were a beautifully
tailored suit. We were going to have to buy time anyways, and
he gave it to us. He could blame himself for the delays. We
concluded the conversation and I called Kellogg, and filled him
in, and tried to persuade him to make the actual buy happen.
He said he couldn't everything was in place. Kellogg told me
that Jose would never see twelve o'clock noon on Wednesday,
May 2, 2001 as a free man.

On May 2, 2001, Wednesday at four A.M. in the morning
approximately three hundred law enforcement officers from
across the valley assembled at the hanger in Visalia, California. This was their designated staging area, or rally point.
At six A.M. many residents were served simultaneously in
order to surprise them while they were vulnerable, and still
tucked snuggly in their beds, and asleep. By serving the warrants early, and simultaneously it would be less likely any of
them could alert any of the others. On this day thirty-two arrest warrants were executed. Forty arrests were made. Ten of

those were Federal Indictments, and were taken to the Fresno County Jail. The rest went to Kings County Jail and caused massive overcrowding.

Kellogg had promised he would call just to let me know how things went. I was in Corcoran when I received the call. The cell phone rang, and I answered it. "Hello," I said. "Tony it is Kellogg. Everything went great with the exception of Jose. When we smashed in the door and entered the house Jose darted out the back door, jumped over the fence, and the neighbor's dog got a hold of him and mauled his arm up. When he ran we sent the K-9 after him. The K-9 went over the fence after him, and got a hold of him also. We took him down to the hospital, had x-rays taken, and had his arm stitched up. Look I have to go Big Bird is in with, oh wait here he is." "Hay Tony I can't chat long everything went well, and I'm in with your buddy Furbee right now.

I got to go I'll call you later," remarked Big Bird. I began to laugh when he told me he was questioning Furbee because I knew he was going to tell it all, and that was great. People began to reveal their contacts, and sources. The numbers continued to mount, and we were on a roll.

CHAPTER EIGHT
SHERIFF'S MEETING

I WAS SCHEDULED for a meeting with Sheriff on Wednesday, May 30, 2001 at 4:00 P.M. The time was near so I got cleaned up, changed clothes, and left for his office. On the way down I could only think what a waste of time it would be. A repeat of the meeting I had with him in 1995. I don't like getting to where I'm going late. I always arrive at my appointments early, and today was no exception. I walked up to the sheriff's secretary sitting at her desk, and greeted her. "Hello Sylvia nice to see you again," I said. Sylvia responded with, "How are you? I'll tell the Sheriff your here." She got up from her desk and went into the sheriff's office. As she came back out she informed, "The sheriff will see you now." I thanked her and headed for the sheriff's office. As I walked in he was standing by his desk, and he extended out his hand. I extended out mine and we shook hands. "How have you been, and how are things going?" He asked. I responded with, "I'm just fine, and things are great." Then he inquired, "How's the family?" In response I said, "The family is doing great." "What can I do for you?" He asked. "Well I'll get right to the point. I came here today to ask you for a weapons permit." I explained. The sheriff eagerly responded with, "You know we have spoken about this before, so what's changed?" That comment rather caught me off guard because I expected him to be aware of my involvement with the FBI. I then realized he wanted to hear it from me, and let me squirm some. He's the type of person who likes playing the mind games, and flexing his muscle. Letting people know that he's the sheriff like we don't already know. After all my son and I worked on his campaign. We walked the precincts knocking on doors, talked to people about voting him in. In addition we put up hundreds of his signs, wrote letters indorsing him, sold and purchased tickets to his fund raisers. I went ahead and presented my case, "Sheriff you're well aware of my involvement with this most recent drug bust. Nothing goes on in this county that you don't know about. Those guys up in Fresno on Federal Warrants, and this bunch locked up in your jail they are here because of the work I did with the Bureau, and you know that." "Well tell me about it." He asked. "Alright I'll make it as brief as possible." I replied. I went ahead and gave him a run down of what happened. "When I decided to do this I told the agents I was working with to come in and tell you, but I didn't want any of the other locals to know." I explained. "Yes they came by and informed me." He replied. "I've got a lot of time and effort into this operation. I got up at all hours of the day, and night." I told him. The Sheriff then responded with, "We had the head guy all wrapped up. We had three buys on him, and ready to take him down. I wanted to take him down right away, but the FBI wanted to wait. I disagreed with them but eventually I gave into them. I was angry because they were dumping drugs on my streets, and it pissed me off." As he said his piece I realized he didn't know what was going on with the case. His guys didn't have three buys on the head guy. They had three buys alright but it was on Sandoval. It was another associate of Jose's, and I knew exactly who he was talking about. There it came out the type of mentality of wanting to take out someone before that someone has been "picked ripe". Just imagine of all that would have been lost had the Sheriff gone and done things his way. "I'm glad you waited. Look at what we reaped. It paid off." I blurted out. The Sheriff responded with, "Tony thank you for what you have done. I just want you to be safe, and I want you to be able to protect your family." To help my case I added, "The two FBI Agents I'm working with are willing to come down here, and meet with you, and share with you my files. They are willing to go over my extensive involvement with this case." "What are their names?" He asked. I went ahead and gave him their real names. I had to think about it a moment because I didn't usually use their real names. I had given them code names just as they had given me, and I used them all the time. In closing the Sheriff informed me, "You know that most of the deputies from 1993 are gone now. We have a lot of new people. I want you to feel free to call us for help. Sylvia would you please bring me a CCW application?" She brought in the application, and left closing the door behind her. Then the Sheriff continued, "Take this application, fill it out, and return it directly, and only to me. No one needs to know anything about this." I went ahead and reminded him, "You know that I've been carrying off and on since 1993?" He responded with, "Yes you told me you were doing that." In addition I added, "If someone really has a desire to shoot someone else they don't need to have a permit to do so. People shoot each other every day and they don't have permits. My mind set isn't to acquire a permit to be able to shoot someone. I'm in a volatile situation now and I really need one in order to carry legally within the law." The Sheriff then asked, "How do you feel the "Civil Commit" will affect you with this application?" In response I said, "It shouldn't affect me one way or the other because it was civil and not criminal." I was given fifteen days jail time, and fined fifteen hundred dollars for contempt of court and placed under arrest in a "Civil Commit" status. My son had been given a traffic ticket for speeding using radar. We decided to contest the ticket. I researched traffic tickets, and found that in order for the city police to use radar within city limits they must have a "Traffic Engineering Survey" on record. The "Traffic Engineering Survey" must have been done, and certified by the state. What the survey does is justifies the speed the police wants to enforce on that particular piece of roadway. Without it the State of California considers the radar controlled area to be a speed trap, illegal, and unenforceable. When at trial the officer who issued the traffic citation will usually testify to his side of the story, and that there is a "Traffic and Engineering Survey" on file with the court.

The court will state for the record that "The court takes notice of the traffic and engineering survey on file." What's wrong with all this some may wonder? First, the officer can't testify to the Traffic and Engineering Survey because he didn't conduct it. Therefore, the testimony of the officer is hearsay and inadmissible. The officer must produce the Survey, and place it into evidence. That requirement has been waived because the court has a file copy. The court must produce that copy if the defendant requests it. In this case my son had requested it and the judge denied. In that instance I stood up and respectfully reminded the judge that the court did need to produce the copy of the survey. The judge told me to sit down and that I could not talk. I sat down as I was told.

In the beginning of the proceedings my son had given him a "Preemptory Challenge". This is a demand that the judge step down because the defendant feels that the judge will not give him a fair trial, and that another judge should hear the case. We felt that the judge wouldn't give my son a fair trial because we had worked on a committee of a lawyer who had run against him in the last election. The "Challenge" was suppose to be served ten days before the trial. We had not done that. Nevertheless, in the true interest of justice he could have stepped down. Another judge would have stepped down and complied with the challenge. It is common knowledge that judges resent common citizens challenging them. Just as this judge they become insulted and very hostile and sometimes overstep their boundaries. Many times they hand out severe punishments. The courts were actually originally designed so that the common person could come and be heard. This judge was clearly functioning at will without knowledge of what he was truly doing. It may be hard to believe but very true.

As my son stood there, and reminded the judge of the "Challenge" the judge cut him off. I then stood back up and asked the judge why hadn't he stepped down? The judge came back with five days in jail, and five hundred dollar fine. After the handcuffs were on me I told him he ran a "bogus court" and he announced ten days in jail, and one thousand dollar fine. I responded with, "And you're a crooked judge." His final words were, "Fifteen days in jail, and fifteen hundred dollar fine." They took me away, and I did my fifteen days and paid the fine. The judge found my son guilty and he was fined $76.00. We later appealed the traffic ticket, and won. The judge was found to have abused his power, and used excessive force by the Judicial Review Council. He was also reprimanded for making a statement to the media. Something judges are not allowed to do. He was also obligated to take me to another judge for review before sentence was carried out. He failed to do that. It was obvious that the judge didn't know what he was doing, and has no true regard for the law.

The conversation between the sheriff and I concluded with him telling me again that he wanted me and my family to be safe and be able to protect ourselves. I thought he was sincere, but he was really lying. He never intended to give me the permit. I filled out the application, turned it in, and waited for several months. The sheriff stalled until the first trial was over, and I had testified to tell me that he wouldn't give me the permit.

CHAPTER NINE
THE HANFORD TRIAL

IT HAD BEEN NINE months since that unforgettable day of May 2, 2001. The news flashes, the television reports, and the newspapers. The largest drug bust in the history of Kings County was announced on television. It was now February 27, 2002, and I was preparing to testify in court at the trials of Rudy, and Alex. They were the only two left from forty others who decided to take it to trial. All the other defendants had pled out instead of going to trial. There were still approximately sixteen being held up in the Fresno Jail on Federal Warrants.

The events of today would be engraved into my memory for ever. The finale in this chapter of life against good, and evil, and prevailing justice was going to be left up to a jury. My testimony was only a small piece to a large puzzle which had to be recorded into evidence. A trial is a procedure which the accused has the right to experience regardless of the outcome.

As I prepared to leave the house dressed in a new sports jacket, dress slacks, and a forty dollar neck tie snuggly around my neck I thought about the possible impact my testimony would have. My mind was in high gear exchanging one thought for another. Eventually reality set in. I began to think about all the people affected by what just these two defendants had done. I thought that it was a very high price for society, and its victims to pay just so these defendants could feed their "negative self esteems". To satisfy their individual greedy cravings, live a life of luxury, nice cars, and women. What negative impact did they have upon the youth within our communities? Those that saw them as role models simply because of the roll of money in their pockets, some twisted sense of success is what it really is. Their rap music glorifies them with contemporary titles of Ballers, Shot Callers, and Drug Lords. What ever you would like to call them they were still poisoning our small world here in little Hanford right under our law enforcement's noses.

I arrived at the court house, took the stairs up to court room 2 only to discover I had to wait until I was called. I was placed into a side waiting room secluded from everyone else. I sat around waiting with Deputy Blue while enjoying a mild mannered conversation with him. It wasn't long before a bailiff opened the door, and informed me I was up. I made my way to the double doors, walked through them, as all heads turned to the rear of the court room from where I was entering. I made my way down the isle, walked by the defense, and prosecution tables, and up to the witness box. The jury was escorted in by another bailiff, and I was sworn in, and finally took my seat. I looked around the court room systematically first beginning at the prosecution's table where Deputy D.A. Nelson was sitting. Over to his right was Special Agent Big Bird. I looked over to the podium, and then in order from right to left was defense counsel Rudy staring at me with cold, glassy eyes. To his right was one of the defendants who's name was also Rudy. As he leaned forward in his seat I could feel the hatred, and anger I felt piercing towards me. Then defense attorney Blakian, he looked at me as though he was trying to figure out a complex math problem he had not yet been instructed on how to negotiate. Finally my eyes came to rest upon Alex the second defendant. I don't know what he was thinking because he sat there with chilling eyes, and a mid size smirk on his face. Perhaps the dummy hadn't figured out he was on trial yet. No, what he was really thinking is his attorney had a surprise for me. My next thought was should I be concerned? I concluded no!

Deputy District Attorney Nelson began with his direct examination of me. It was question after question, revisiting past occurrences. After a couple of hours with him Defense Attorneys Blakian, and Rudy openly discussed who would question me next. They decided Blake would take his jabs at me. He came right at me like some bull charging out of a rodeo chute. You would have thought that he would bee more strategic, and methodical when approaching me. He asked me the same questions multiple times. I began to wonder why Deputy DA Nelson wasn't objecting. Then I remembered a comment he had made the first day we had met. "I have the mind to put you on the stand and allow the defense attorneys just rip you up." It all made sense. Nelson never objected. The judge became frustrated, and scolded Mr. Blakian three times. As Mr. Blakian continued with his line of questioning the judge found it necessary to stop the proceedings, had the jury removed from the court room, and proceeded to reprimand Mr. Blakian. The jury was brought back in, and we proceeded on. Mr. Blakian read to me two pages of reports written by Special Agent Big Bird. The reports were created from information which I had provided directly to Big Bird. As Mr. Blakian concluded the reading of the reports he began to scold me, and asked why I hadn't reported this information to the FBI. He caught me by surprise because at first I really didn't understand what he was asking. The most I could figure out was that it was an effort to try and make me look incompetent, or dirty me up in some way. I became angry due to his own confused mind and responded, "Those two pages of reports were written by Special Agent Big Bird, I agree, but the information in those reports came into being because I gave Special Agent Big Bird that specific information." Again he repeated the accusations of failing to report to the FBI, and referred to the two pages of reports. I responded by raising my voice, "What do mean? Those two pages of reports were created because I gave the agents that information, and that is how those two pages came to be." As I finished my sentence I looked over at the prosecution table at Deputy D.A. Nelson in frustration. I had been waiting for him to object to the line of questioning but it didn't come. I knew at that moment he was a weak prosecutor and I was on my own. As a second thought in my opinion I felt that he was probably under orders to allow them to badger as much as possible. Blakian looked at me with what seemed to be an embarrassed look on his face as though he had just realized what mistake he had just made. No telling what he was really thinking in that brain of his? Wow was this guy out there! He then walked over to his table placed the two reports down, and continued on with a different line of questioning. I began to think Mr. Blakian was really stupid, but that wasn't the case at all. I think he had a little trouble getting started perpetuated with the fact that his client had lied to him. Mr. Blakian had been given information he thought he could impeach me with. His client Alex kept that smirk on his face for the longest time, and I could see he was enjoying every moment of the offensive. When he realized that his planned ambush hadn't worked Alex's facial expression changed to one of deep concern. Before the trials all the defendants had been offered plea bargains before my name was released during the discovery phase. Perhaps Alex was now thinking he should have taken the plea bargain, but it was too late now. It was a high stakes roll of the dice, and he would have had better odds in Las Vegas.

Mr. Blakian went on and continued to ask me if I had ever campaigned for County Supervisor? I responded with, "Yes." Mr. Blakian followed up with, "Didn't you receive a substantial amount of money as a campaign donation from Jose M, and Ceasar C? I never had received money from them and responded to the question in the same. Mr. Blakian went on with, "Didn't Ceasar place campaign bumper stickers on all his vehicles?" "Yes that is true. Those bumper stickers were on my counter top in my store and were free for the taking. What was I suppose to do grab the bumper stickers from his hand, and tell him no." Blakian went ahead and concluded for the moment and turned it over to the other defense attorney Rudy. Defense Attorney Rudy was of Philippine origin, in his mid or late seventies. He was very emotional and theatrical during his few moments of fame. He didn't appear to be too quick, but I wasn't sure if he was trying to throw me off guard so I would be unprepared for round two. It really didn't matter because my intentions were to just tell the truth. The session was brief, and I thought to be rather insignificant. Once he indicated he was through I was asked to step down off the witness stand, and the judge informed me that I was subject to recall. As I stepped off, and walked down the isle I noticed the local newspaper reported in the court room. I knew there would be some mention of the trial in the newspaper. On the way home I stopped off to purchase a copy of the newspaper. Surprisingly enough on the top, right front page in bold lettering was **"Star Witness Takes Stand In Drug Trial"**.

The weekend had passed, and Monday morning, the fourth of March was upon me. I had woken up early, it was five A.M. and I felt a little tense. I washed up, got dressed, and went off to do my dairy supply route has I have routinely done for the past nineteen years. I quickly got through the route, and made it back to the house to wait for the call. I fell asleep watching television, and my cell phone buzzed. I answered, and it was Kellogg, "Tony I need you to come down to the court house I think you'll be going on the stand next." In response, "Are you sure it's almost lunch time. The judge will probably want to break for lunch." I sensed Kellogg beginning to get tense as he snapped, "I don't know for sure but hurry, and get here as quickly as you can." "OK," I blurted out with discontent. I rushed into the bathroom shaved quickly, and jumped into the shower. I was dressed into my sport jacket, and tie in about five minutes, and ready to go. I was about eighteen minutes away from the court house depending on traffic. It was 11:38 when I arrived at the court house. My anticipated wait lasted only about fifteen minutes when we got word that we would be breaking for lunch, and there was talk that the judge was considering throwing out the "wire taps". We came back from lunch, and waited until 1:00 P.M. for court to resume. It wasn't until 2 P.M. when we got word that the "wire taps" were on their way out. As a second year law student I knew how crucial these wire taps were. They implicated a whole lot of people and established various elements to the over all scope of the case. Apparently the defense team argued technicalities of the "wire taps qualifying as evidence. They seemed to have had a better, and more convincing argument that the prosecution. Quickly Kellogg and a couple of other investigators scrambled for their cell phones. They were calling Bakersfield, and locating the state's most qualified expert in the area of "wire taps". The "wire taps" were crucial to this case because it would establish the continued conspiracies involving the drug trafficking, and manufacturing. In all their efforts they had located "Tam" the "wire tap"expert, and they had arranged to get an airplane in the air with "Tam" aboard, airborne, and headed for the Hanford Airport. It all took place, and came together in a matter of a few minutes. They were in the court room with "Tam" in forty-five minutes. What an incredible display of team work, dedication, effort, and precision. "Tam took the stand, testified, and the judge allowed in the testimony, and the "wire tap" evidence. Monday was coming to a close. I expressed my dissatisfaction with the waste of my time having to sit around. After all I could have been studying at home, and without distractions since I was in law school. I expressed my feelings to Deputy D.A. Nelson, and informed him I would not come in on Tuesday until he was certain I would be taking the stand. I couldn't afford to waste any more precious study time. The numerous investigators who were in from Bakersfield, and waiting around were also expressing their dissatisfaction, and blaming it on the judge. The judge could have avoided these delays involving the questions at hand about the "wire taps". After all they did have trial readiness hearings, and the attorneys could have been informed then. This of course would have ignited a flood of motions between the defense team, and the prosecution. Considering the waste of valuable man hours which could have been better spent catching dangerous drug dealers.

As court went into recess until tomorrow I headed for home with a sheriff escort following close behind. I pulled into my driveway, and my escort broke off tooting his horn. I dressed into a pair of jeans, t-shirt, sat down and tried to relax as I waited for dinner. Not more than ten minutes and my cell phone went off. It was Kellogg, "Tony I want you to, well it's more of a request, I was wondering if you could come down to the DA's Office right now, and go over the "wire taps". My reply was, "Sure no problem I'll be right down." I left almost immediately, and arrived a few minutes later. I entered through the side door as I had been instructed to do. As I received my instructions, and got ready to begin listening to the recordings Big Bird, and Nelson discovered that the recordings were securely left back in the court room with some of the other evidence. Not able to authenticate the accuracy of the transcripts, and the recordings my job there was completed before it had gotten started. We all agreed that there was nothing for me to do so I prepared to leave, and in doing so Nelson requested I arrive at the court house no later than 8:00 A.M. the following morning. I wasn't sure if he wanted me to come straight to the court house at eight, or report to the DA's Office next door. The next words out of Nelson's mouth would infuriate me for the next twelve hours. Adam replied, "Don't come here because you're not welcome here. Report to the court house tomorrow at eight A.M. and I'll meet you there. I agreed, and left angry with that statement causing my blood to boil. I felt the statement was uncalled for. Although, I realized that the statement was true.

The reasoning behind the comment was driven from an incident which had occurred in1993. Eric one of the investigators in the office had a special dislike for me because my family and I had won a judgment against him for his part in arresting us for holding down intruders. In addition the chief deputy district attorney who was involved in the case in 1993 was back and gainfully employed in that same office. He too had a great dislike for me because he had been named in a separate suit for which the county settled with us out of court. I assume that they probably expressed their desire that I not be allowed in the building even though I was the star prosecution witness. Big Bird has assured me though out this ordeal that I can trust local law enforcement and the DA's Office. He continues to reassure me every time we get together. In rebuttal I try and convince him that I can't trust them. My reasons are well established from comments and through their present day actions. Perhaps one day he will understand and see things the way they truly are.

Twelve hours had passed, and Tuesday was well on my door step. I got myself ready and headed down to the court house. I arrived five minutes before anyone else, and entered into the adjacent waiting rooms where we had been waiting the day before. Nelson arrived shortly after I did, and began setting up the CD player, and brought out the transcripts. He looked at me and commented that I looked upset. I responded in the affirmative. He asked, "What's the matter?" I replied, "It was what you said last night. What do you mean I'm not welcome? A few weeks ago when you first stated that I disregarded it and paid no mind. Last night you summoned me down there, and I felt you just wanted to wipe my face in that comment like you got some pleasure out of it. Who's policy is that, I'm not welcome down at the DA's Office?" Nelson looked at me with a surprised look on his face, and attempted to explain, "Well you know how some people feel about you down at the office because of your lawsuit against the county years ago. You're taking it all out of context. No one established that policy, and I apologize for upsetting you." "Alright," I said. When I heard the "Your taking out of context" it just ticked me off, and goes to show he was doing some back tracking, and looking for an excuse. That is what people say when placed on the defensive and can't come up with a more intellectual response. It's like the cat caught in the act with the canary in its mouth. With that comment he was throwing it back on me. He was insulting my intelligence trying to say I didn't understand what he was say-ing. In response I say, "On the contrary my dear Watson!"

My cell phone began to buzz. I answered it and Big Bird's voice came over the air waves, "Hay we'll be there in a few minutes, I didn't over sleep if that's what your thinking." That's exactly what I was thinking, or perhaps he had to make a "Krispy Kreme donut stop? "O K see ya when you get here," I blurted out.

Kellogg, and Big Bird finally arrived. Immediately following, Blue got there with informant Jesse. Blue, and Jesse went off and sat in another waiting room. They wanted to keep us apart. After all Jesse's testimony was being traded for accepting a plea bargain. Instead of doing ten years he would do five a generous trade off in exchange. I thought they shouldn't have done a plea offer with Jesse. Nelson should have let him do the ten years. The evidence against him was damning enough, and I don't believe his testimony against the defendants made a difference. The only real advantage was to avoid another trial which involved time and money as I saw it. I was finally off and running. I was listening to the "wire taps" and reading along with the transcripts checking that they both matched for accuracy. I went through both sets of CDs, and transcripts, and found no discrepancies. I clearly identified, and recognized the voices that were on the recording. The voices were those of several of the defendants that had been arrested, and my voice as well.

It was ten minutes to twelve, and we were all getting ready to go to lunch. Before I left for lunch Nelson reassured me that perhaps I would take the stand again after lunch. I went to lunch alone and enjoyed a combo meal at Wendy's while I thought about some of the events that had taken place which brought us here to court. My thoughts were not of anything specific, but more in general. I made my way back to the court house, and waited. Sure enough I was called just as Nelson had promised. I walked into the court room, and went directly up to the witness stand. The jury was not yet present. Everyone was now back, present, and awaiting for the judge to call in the jury. I sat back in my chair, and watch the attorneys talking among themselves. Suddenly in a loud voice as if to intentionally draw attention to himself Attorney Rudy blurted out, "I like this jury instruction!" (directing attention to an 8 by 10 inch piece of white paper) "It says that any person Attorney Rudy defends is automatically not guilty." I couldn't help myself and nearly choked on laughter I was trying to regain control. Everyone quieted down, and the judge ordered the jury to come in. Everyone came to their feet as the bailiff escorted in the jury.

While on the witness stand Nelson commenced to question me about the "wire tape recordings. The reason for the process was to authenticate the matching of the CD's recording of the "wire taps" and matching the voices to the typed transcripts. Nelson finished with his line of questioning, and the judge began to ask me questions. Judge Shultz asked me specifically for each CD and transcript if in fact I had found any discrepancies, between what was said and what the transcript had in print. I responded, "No there are none." He then went further to ask me if specifically, each printed initial to the right of the printed quotes in the transcripts matched the identity of the person speaking on the CD. I responded, "Yes they match." The judge was finished, and allowed Attorney Rudy to commence with his questioning.

Attorney Rudy began right in with the "wire tap" recordings. He asked me, "How many times have you listened to the tapes?" I responded, "Three or four times, three times I believe." Rudy asked, "When was the first time?" "About six weeks ago at the Fresno Field Office," I replied. Rudy then asked, "When was the second time? "Yesterday," I said. Rudy continued to ask, "When was the last time?" "This morning at eight o'clock," I replied. Then Rudy asked, "Did you inspect the CDs, and match them for the correct evidence tags, and numbers?" (each CD recording of the wire taps were all labeled with individual evidence stickers so that they could be recorded into evidence, and identified) I answered, "Yes I did match evidence tag 54 to its CD and 54A to its transcript. Also 55 to its CD and 55A to its transcript, and they each matched."Rudy asked, "Oh so you listened to the recording at five this morning?" My response was, "No I said at eight this morning." Rudy then stated, "Oh I must be having trouble hearing. So at five this morning you listened to the recording?" Becoming very irritated I put my lips close to the microphone, and in a loud voice I said, "Yes you must be loosing your hearing because I told you it was at eight this morning." Rudy then asked, "You say you verified the evidence numbers of the CDs, how can that be if they were just placed on them this morning (close to yelling)?" I was thrown off guard with his comment because I didn't expect him to lie. I thought about it a moment. I responded irritated once again, "I did inspect, and match the evidence numbers, and verified them to match." Rudy then stated, "Alright, I'm finished with the witness your honor." Attorney Rudy then took his seat at the defense table.

Mr. Blakian had been "lying in wait" for me like a tiger crouched down and anxiously awaiting his moment of attack. He began, "Do you know Paul Sandoval?" I replied, "Yes I do." Blakian then asked, "Tell me how you know him." I then responded, "He's a drug dealer, and part of the Magana Drug Ring." Then Blake asked, "Paul Sandoval use to patronize your store is that correct?" I answered, "Yes that is correct." Blakian then impatiently asked, "He use to come in and purchase MSM isn't that right?" I again responded with, "Yes that is right he did." The questions came quicker. Blakian then asked, "You had a close relationship with him didn't you?" I quickly blurted out, "No I did not!" I had felt insulted by that question. Then Blakian came to where he wanted to be and asked, "You in fact had a close relationship with him that you co-signed so he could buy a car isn't that right?" I immediately responded with, "No that is false and it never happened!" Blakian asked, "If he came into this court room and testified under oath that you did would that be a lie?" "That's right he would be lying!" I said. I was thinking that perhaps this line of questioning was a prep period, and all he was trying to do was trying to get warmed up. I looked deep beyond his obvious facial expressions, and found deep in through his eyes the look of a desperate attorney trying to conceal panic. His line of questioning seemed to be searching for flaws or inconsistencies in my testimony. Apparently there were none because the questioning ceased. Nevertheless, he succeeded in doing what he set out to do and that was cause confusion among the jurors. I went ahead and stepped down from the stand, and was able to leave. I went home, and got myself ready for class. As I took the very familiar forty-five minute drive to school I couldn't help but revisit some of the questions Blakian asked. They weren't really significant in the least.

I wasn't in class more than twenty minutes, and my cell phone buzzed. I could see into the sight glass that it was Kellogg's number. I answered hello, "Look I really don't know how to say this, but we have information that there is a possible hit out on you. Some guys coming up from Mexico," said Kellogg. I then asked, "Where did this information come from?" Kellogg in response, "We got information out of the jail, we have an informant in there. You need to be careful." Blue got on the phone next, and lectured me not to do anything stupid, don't go outside if they come to your house. You need to stay inside and call me. I'll get there as soon as possible and I'll have back up rolling. I agreed, and concluded the conversation. I went back into the classroom, and excused myself, and headed for home. I had to get home as quickly as possible informing my family of the possible threat. I didn't want to warn them over the phone. I wanted to do it in a calm and controlled manner so as not to cause panic or chaos. I got home, broke the news to my family. They began to become extremely upset but simmered down when I said that right now we all needed to be careful. The information had not yet been confirmed whether it was for real, or just a couple of irritated, and angry jail inmates on trial.

Wednesday came and went with no excitement. Everything began to wind down in one aspect but on the other hand things were about to gear up for closing arguments.

Thursday arrived and I got to the court house at ten A.M.. Closing statements began with Nelson. I didn't think Nelson's closing was all that good. He took a couple of hours and he was through. He was going to get a second bite of the apple later once the defense was through. I thought perhaps he saved his best for then.

Defense Attorney Rudy got up, stood at the podium, and began with his closing. It was a fiasco I thought. He was all over the board. First he talked about Marylyn Monroe (it was obvious he was obsessed with her) and how he came here to America from the Philippines. He talked about America's beautiful mountains, and its greenery. He then sang a short tune, and people were amused. I was beginning to wonder if I hadn't wondered into the wrong building or something. His closing was terrible, and I thought Defendant Rudy should have gotten a refund. Attorney Rudy tried to play off his client as though he was a poor drug addict in need of treatment, and not punishment. His client was dangerous, and needed to be locked up for a long time. Before the trial began Defendant Rudy was offered a plea bargain of two to four years. He rejected it, rolled the dice and went to trial. He now faced a maximum of twelve years. Attorney Rudy insulted and attacked our beloved FBI agents. He tried several times to discredit them, but it didn't seem to work. It was soon over, and Blakian was up to bat.

The clock was ticking, and time was flying by. Blakian took his position on the floor of the court room, and began. He didn't dare insult, or try to discredit the FBI Agents. In fact he applauded them for a job well done. He didn't attack Blue as Rudy had done. He focused in on me, and began in a desperate attempt to tear me down. In a last clear chance to save his client, a dangerous drug dealer, trafficker, and member of a very large drug ring. He began with, "Mr. Araujo is responsible for taking out a large drug ring, and taking large amounts of drugs off the streets. Thank God because there will be many children that now these drugs won't harm." Blakian went on to say shifting his approach, "His testimony is not credible, as he was motivated by the promise of immunity in his sales of MSM to members of the local drug culture, as well as an FBI payment of $35,000.00 for his help." Blake continued to say, "Araujo is dangerous. I think that Araujo is a bigger conspirator than these defendants. Araujo is a selfish man who cares only about himself. He did what he did to keep himself from jail."

I was hurt, and had to sit there listening to this garbage unable to defend myself because it would have been wrong to do so, and interrupt the process. I knew and, expected the attack. Nevertheless, it was painful because it wasn't true, and he was lying. After all it was the FBI that recruited me. He didn't want to just cut me down. His intentions were to totally destroy me.

He wanted to trade me in exchange for his client. One thing I was not was selfish or greedy. Looking at the bright side as they were, Blakian in all his emotions did implicate his client in his comparison to me being a much larger conspirator than his client Alex. Hopefully the jury caught that admission of guilt. I had to leave shortly there after, and the closing arguments continued hammering away at my credibility. If it were true that I only thought of myself then why would I put myself in harms way? My history clearly displays my concern for others and my desire to help my fellow man. He attempted to place me on trial and divert his client's guilt. Again he was successful in confusing the jurors.

When Deputy D. A. Nelson got up for his final closing he only came to my defense once, and said, "If Araujo's actions were criminal for his part in continuing to sell MSM to people he knew were involved in the local drug culture - then it would make no sense that Araujo voluntarily submitted information to the FBI in the first place." Nelson went on to say that, "Mr. Araujo isn't on trial here."

The day of reckoning had arrived. The day we had patiently waited for. It was Friday, March 8th, 2002. The jury would get the case today and a win or loose for the good guys would come soon enough. I kept busy between my Dairy Supply Business and law books. It was 4:30 P.M. and I decided to call Big Bird. The phone rang several times, and no answer. He must be in court I thought. I called Kellogg, and thought if he doesn't answer he must also be in court awaiting a jury verdict. Suddenly after two rings Kellogg picked up. I asked, "Hay have you heard anything yet?" "Yes in fact we have. The jury asked that if they had agreed on just one, if they could report their verdict?" answered Kellogg. "Well what happened?" I asked. Kellogg responded, "The verdict on Rudy was guilty on all counts. They still don't have a decision on Alex." We concluded our conversation and each of us hung up. What a sad day for the Rudy family I thought. Although I was pleased with the verdict I thought what a waste of a young life. It was truly a victory for us but there was no celebration for me. Rudy received twelve years the maximum allowed by law for his activities within the Magana Organization. On the bright side this fellow was extremely dangerous, and was going to be placed securely away where he couldn't hurt the innocent, and defenseless. Who was to blame? It appeared that perhaps his family lacked giving him the proper up bringing? Could it have been a failure to instill family values, religious values or both? Obviously it was some environmental influence that caused him to become what he was. Rudy had a child of his own, and how would all this affect this child? I felt that all those long hours, and hard work paid off for me and all of the other law enforcement people that were involved. The ultimate victory was for those unborn and defenseless children which would have become casualties of this dangerous predator through his sales and support of this dangerous organization.

Monday March 11, 2002 had arrived. I was looking forward to the jurors making up their minds on Alex. It was 2:00 P.M. and I was hard at work on my computer in my office working on a law essay. My cell phone buzzed, it caught me by surprise, and I jumped about two inches off my chair. It was Big Bird. I immediately asked, "I hope you have good news." He responded, "No I surely don't. The jury let Alex walk on all counts. One of the jurors said that the evidence on Alex was not as strong as it was on Rudy." I replied, "That was a stupid way to look at it, I can't believe it. It won't be long until he's back doing his drug dealings." Blakian had done his job he had gotten his client of. He had created enough confusion and division among the jurors. Big Bird had asked one of the jurors if they had listened to the tape recordings. The juror agreed that there was no doubt that the voice was that of Alex's. The juror insisted that the measure of evidence were not the same. That is what they based it on. Although that is not how they should have decided guilt or innocence.

There was in fact overwhelming evidence against Rudy. Although the amount of evidence on Alex was not as much there was still more than enough to convict him on at least something. That is the risk the prosecution takes when they try and cut corners and bring two defendants together at trial. Besides I don't believe Nelson did a good enough job at trial. He was rather passive. He allowed the defense attorneys to try and toy with me. I was very much on my own. I suppose that was a punishment for suing the county in 1993. Nelson gave it away during our first meeting. He had said that he had the mind to let me go it alone when I took the stand. I suppose that was supposed to scare me.

On February 27, 2003 I received word that Jose had received fifteen years of a plea bargain. He was originally facing twenty-five to life. Lucky him I guess. The immense desire for "fueling his negative self-esteem" had just cost him fifteen years of his life. In return for his much lower sentence Jose had cooperated with the FBI. His information led to further arrests.

On approximately July 8, 2003 the FBI presented me with an award for my participation in this operation. It was with great pride that I accepted the award and happy to have served my country and my community.

COMMENTS

WHEN THE KINGS County Sheriff was approached by the FBI and was informed of the operation the sheriff wanted to arrest all the suspects immediately and bring it all to an end. This would have caused the operation to fail, and allow many of the drug dealers to remain on the streets conducting their business as usual. It wasn't until Wednesday, May 2, 2001 that the Sheriff's Office joined the drug task force unit, known as High Intensity Drug Trafficking Area Task Force (HIDTA) for short. Joining the HIDTA was a great benefit to the community because it poured in massive resources from the Federal and State levels. Which otherwise would have taken several years to accomplish what was done in nine months with limited local resources.

It is now clear to the FBI that allowing Paul Sandoval to plea bargain out, and placed into the State's Witness Protection Program was a mistake. His testimony was not instrumental in the conviction of the defendants whom he testified against. The only real event which he was responsible for was executing a controlled buy on Huerta who until now has not been mentioned. Paul had two strikes against him, and with this one being his third he would have been facing life. Even after I warned the locals not to give him a break because he couldn't be trusted they went ahead and did it anyway. It appears to me that the state funds wasted to keep Paul on the "Program" has been a mismanagement of taxpayer dollars. The State Witness Protection Program was designed to protect a witness which gave valuable, and valid testimony. In other words information that was incriminating, and damaging to the magnitude which warranted the implementation of the program. In this case the value of the testimony and the assistance provided failed to weigh out on a comparative scale. In other words he cheated the District Attorney's Office because they are the ones who would have offered him and approved the program. Sandoval regurgitated information which he read from reports, information which was not known or unaware by law enforcement. Again because local law enforcement lacks sophistication and desire to exert the needed efforts and resources Sandoval was able to take advantage and maneuver himself into the program with tax payers flipping the bill. Sandoval's testimony was not needed and was more of a liability than a supposed asset.

This book is dedicated to those children who have become victim to the causes and affects of the illicit drug culture.

APPENDIX

DEPARTMENT OF THE ARMY
SAN FRANCISCO FIELD OFFICE, SIXTH REGION
US ARMY CRIMINAL INVESTIGATION COMMAND
PRESIDIO OF SAN FRANCISCO, CALIFORNIA 94129

CIRFS   24 February 1975

SUBJECT: Letter of Appreciation

SP4 Antonio Araujo

San Francisco, CA

1. During the period 10 Dec 74 - 21 Jan 75, you assisted this office in
the successful investigation of drug related offenses. Your efforts were
significant in the identification and apprehension of three dealers of
illicit drugs and the confiscation of a substantial amount of the illicit
drug.

2. I take this opportunity to commend you for the approach you have taken
toward your duties as a member of this military community and as a concerned
citizen. As Commander of the San Francisco Field Office, Sixth Region,
USACIDC, Presidio of San Francisco, CA, I extend to you the sincere appreciation of this office.

JAMES R CRINAN
MAJ, MPC
Commanding

DEPARTMENT OF THE ARMY
SAN FRANCISCO FIELD OFFICE, 6TH REGION
US ARMY CRIMINAL INVESTIGATION COMMAND
PRESIDIO OF SAN FRANCISCO, CALIFORNIA 94129

CIRFS   9 December 1974

SUBJECT: Letter of Appreciation

Antonio A. ARAUJO

HHC, United States Army Garrison
Presidio of San Francisco, CA 94129

1. The San Francisco Field Office, extends great appreciation to SP4 Antonio A. ARAUJO for providing information that led to the successful investigation and recovery of stolen Army ID Cards, without which the aforementioned stolen ID Cards may have fallen into the wrong hands and subsequently used to commit crimes against the US Army and US Government.

2. Many thanks for your timely cooperation. What you did is in keeping with the finest tradition of the military service and reflects great credit upon yourself and the United States Army.

R W White

ROBERT W. WHITE
Special Agent
San Francisco Field Office

FD-302 (Rev. 10-6-95)

- 1 -

FEDERAL BUREAU OF INVESTIGATION

Date of transcription   09/24/2000

On 09/22/00, directly following a controlled purchase of approximately four pounds of methamphetamine, a Source, who is in a position to testify, was interviewed by writers regarding the details of the purchase. Also present was Bureau of Narcotics Enforcement (BNE) Special Agent Alfred Frausto. Source provided the following information:

Source drove to JOSE MAGANA's old house at the corner of Excelsior and 15th Avenues in Hanford, California and pulled up to the property. Source observed a red Honda parked under the sun shade and also a black Camaro or Firebird parked at the property. Source removed a ten pound bucket of MSM from his vehicle and knocked on the door Two individuals came to the door. One was an unidentified white male, approximately 5' 9" tall, 170 pounds, unshaven with blond hair in his forties. The other individual was a young Mexican male, short, approximately 140 pounds, with dark, well-groomed hair whom Source recognized as MAGANA's cousin. The white male exited the residence as if he was leaving and walked past the Source. He appeared to be nervous to been seen by the Source. Source followed MAGANA's cousin into the residence and into the kitchen. Source heard noises in the back of the house and asked MAGANA's cousin if anyone else was there. MAGANA's cousin replied that the noises were trucks passing by the house on the street. Source asked MAGANA's cousin where the methamphetamine was. MAGANA's cousin said, "It's right here." and pointed to a brown paper grocery bag on the kitchen counter containing four, 10 to 12 inch long, cylindrical bundles of an off-white substance wrapped in clear plastic cellophane. Source asked MAGANA's cousin how much was there. MAGANA's cousin responded, "Four pounds." Source asked if the bundles were one pound each and handed one of the bundles to MAGANA's cousin. MAGANA's cousin stated that they were and handed the bundle back to the Source. Source placed the bundle back in the grocery bag. Source told MAGANA's cousin that he had the money in his vehicle outside. Source exited the residence and retrieved a white plastic bag containing $11,200 in cash provided to the Source by the writers. Source noticed that the black Camaro or Firebird was now gone and Source assumed that the unidentified white male had left in the vehicle. Source brought the money back inside the residence, handed it to MAGANA's cousin and told him he could count it. Source asked MAGANA's

Investigation on   09/22/00   at Hanford, California

File # 270P-SC-34351, 281C-SC-34347   Date dictated

by

- 1 -

FEDERAL BUREAU OF INVESTIGATION

Date of transcription   10/02/2000

On 09/28/2000, directly following a controlled purchase of approximately one pound of methamphetamine and three ounces of rock cocaine, a Source, who is in a position to testify, was interviewed by writers regarding the details of the purchase. Also present was Bureau of Narcotics Enforcement (BNE) Special Agent ███████████. Source provided the following information:

Source drove to JOSE MAGANA's old house at the corner of Excelsior and 15th Avenues in Hanford, California and pulled up to the property. Source observed a red Honda parked at the house and read off the license plate. Source took a ten pound bucket of MSM from his vehicle and walked up to the porch. On the porch, Source observed approximately 12 one-gallon containers of denatured alcohol and two gray, five-gallon containers of an unidentified substance. MAGANA's cousin who had sold Source four pounds of methamphetamine on 09/22/2000, came to the door. MAGANA's cousin said something to the effect of, "Your ears must have been ringing because Jose wanted to know where you're at." Source followed MAGANA's cousin into the house and to the kitchen. Source observed a white, plastic bucket on the kitchen counter. MAGANA's cousin said, "It's all here." Source opened the lid of the bucket and observed four packages of an off-white substance wrapped in clear plastic and one clear plastic baggie containing several pieces of a white, rock-like substance. Source went outside to Source's vehicle and retrieved a white plastic bag containing $5,600 in cash provided to the Source by the writers. Source told MAGANA's cousin that he only wanted one pound of methamphetamine and the rock cocaine and told him to tell MAGANA to hold on to the rest of the drugs for Source for tomorrow and not to sell them. Source counted out $4,220 in cash and then counted the money again. Source owed $4,225 for the drugs ($2,800 for the pound of methamphetamine and $475 for each ounce of rock cocaine), but he only counted out $4,220 because Source didn't have any five dollar bills. MAGANA's cousin tried to take the money before Source was done counting and Source told him to wait until Source was done. MAGANA's cousin removed three of the packages from the bucket and put them under the kitchen counter. Source told MAGANA's cousin again to make sure he didn't sell the drugs and exited the residence. Source drove directly to the staging point, handed the bucket over to writers, and showed writers the $450 given back to Source as

---

Investigation on   09/28/2000   at   Hanford, California

File #   ████████████████████████████   Date dictated

by

uation of FD-302 of _____ Source _____ , On __09/28/2000__ , Page __2__

payment for the MSM. Source advised that MAGANA's cousin said his
name was "CHRIS".

- 1 -

FEDERAL BUREAU OF INVESTIGATION

Date of transcription   10/02/2000

On 09/29/2000, directly following a controlled purchase of approximately one half pound of methamphetamine, a Source, who is in a position to testify, was interviewed by writers regarding the details of the purchase. Source provided the following information:

Several minutes before Source arrived at the Excelsior address, JOSE MAGANA called Source and told Source that he was ready to make the deal. As Source drove up 15th Avenue, he noticed MAGANA's red Dodge pick-up truck heading eastbound on Excelsior Avenue. Source drove to the residence on Excelsior and pulled up to the property. Source observed a red Honda parked at the house and read off the license plate. As Source walked up to the residence, MAGANA's cousin CHRIS opened the door to the bedroom. Source followed CHRIS into the kitchen. CHRIS removed a white plastic MSM bucket from the refrigerator and showed it to Source. Source observed three packages of an off-white substance wrapped in clear plastic inside. CHRIS took the packages from the bucket and laid them on the counter. Source asked CHRIS if he had three ounces of rock cocaine and CHRIS replied, "Not here we don't." Source heard a knock on the door. Source asked CHRIS who was at the door and CHRIS answered, "Someone I've been waiting for." CHRIS went to answer the door and Source told CHRIS not to open the door with the drugs laying out on the counter. CHRIS said, "It's cool." Source told CHRIS it wasn't okay. CHRIS closed the folding door between the kitchen and bedroom and went to the door. CHRIS returned to the kitchen and Source asked CHRIS if he could get half a pound of methamphetamine. CHRIS removed another plastic bucket from the refrigerator with a baggie inside of it containing a block of an off-white substance. CHRIS broke off approximately half of the block and weighed it on a scale in the kitchen. CHRIS put the substance in a baggie and dropped it in a brown paper bag for Source. Source told CHRIS that Source forgot the money in Source's vehicle. Source exited the residence to retrieve the money. Source observed the same unshaven, blond, white male outside that Source had seen on 09/22/2000. The white male was acting like he was working on a moped in the back of the house. Source also observed a black Camaro parked in the driveway. Source retrieved a brown paper McDonald's bag containing $1,380 in cash provided to Source by writers and returned to the residence. Source gave the

---

restigation on   09/29/2000   at Hanford, California

File # ███████████████████████████   Date dictated ....

by ....

uation of FD-302 of   Source   , On 09/29/2000 , Page   2

money to CHRIS and took the bag of methamphetamine. Source asked
CHRIS if JOSE wanted any more MSM. CHRIS said he didn't think so.
As Source exited the residence, CHRIS said, "Be careful." Source
returned to Source's vehicle and read off the license plate of the
black Camaro. Source then drove directly to the staging point, and
handed over the bag of methamphetamine to writers.

Case shows level of sophistication in drug trade

By Amy Tunison
Sentinel Staff Writer

HANFORD — The arrest of Jose Pastor Magana, suspected to be one of the largest methamphetamine manufacturers and traffickers in California, is an example of how much more sophisticated the drug trade — and the law enforcement that polices it — has become.

"It's run just like a normal organization, it's like a business in structure," Cmdr. Mike Ortiz, a 16-year veteran of narcotics in law enforcement and head of the Kings County Narcotics Task Force, said.

"Magana was the president of the organization," he said.

The NTF was pivotal in the recent raid on the Hanford-based Magana organization. Working with state, federal and local law enforcement, it has made over 20 arrests of prominent members of the business.

"Our game plan now is to attack organizations, not individuals," he said. "If we can take the structure down, then the organization is erased."

Ortiz said there are two kinds of drug trafficking organizations, or DTOs, family and nonfamily based.

Magana's organization was family based, according to Ortiz, where family members such as brothers, uncles, sisters and cousins hold key positions of power in the upper echelons to maintain the organization.

"This tends to insulate it from law enforcement because if a member is arrested it is nearly impossible to get information from individuals because they aren't going to snitch on family," Ortiz said.

"Organizations like that can

See CASE; Page 12

Ortiz said the hard work that led to the final arrests was gratifying.

"It's very satisfying," Ortiz said of the arrest. "Because it's something we've been investigating for over a year, and nine months with the FBI."

There was also frustration.

For the most part they had to sit and watch Magana's organization go about its business, gathering evidence to make their case. Any whiff that the law was on to them, such as an unusual number of arrests of Magana's lieutenants for minor drug charges, would have tipped their hand to Magana's organization, according to Ortiz.

"That's a lot of time, looking at what's going on and watching what's going on and not being able to take action against individuals because we're targeting the whole organization," he said. "Patience is sometimes a bitter pill to swallow."

Ortiz said that if nothing else, he hopes the local law enforcement has sent a message to anyone who would want to pick up where Magana left off.

"However, greed of money is a strong motivator," Ortiz said. "So I'm sure at some point, some organization will try to fill that void."

"As we take down organizations we get important insight into how they operated," he said. "The more insight we have the easier it is to identify and impact those organizations."

"We get smarter," he said. "And they get smarter too. It's a chess game."

The reporter can be reached at atunison@sentinelnews.net

Case

Continued from Page 1

take hits, unless we can attack it as a whole," he said.

Ortiz said that in all his years in narcotics, Magana's organization was probably the most violent.

"I've dealt with several and this makes the top of my list as being violent," Ortiz said. "Our intelligence shows that many threats were made towards people in and out of the organization."

Another example of the potential for violence were the amount of weapons seized during the sweep.

"Over 40 weapons were seized, there were weapons at these residences," he said. "Maybe it's due to Jose's youth, but he wielded a big stick and made many threats."

"His method of getting things done was to strong-arm," Ortiz said. "He was not unwilling to use violence."

Ortiz said that Kings and Tulare counties could be considered safer now that Ortiz and much of his organization have been arrested.

"Very much so, Magana had a strong hold on the meth trade, and a lot of seizures we've made we've tied back to the Magana organization," he said.

Like any business, Magana had departments and department heads.

"He had divisions," Ortiz said. "Some who only handled cocaine, some who only handled marijuana, and some that only handled methamphetamine."

"We were able to identify those tentacles," he said, which helped in surveillance.

FRIDAY, MAY 4, 2001
The Sentinel
Hanford, California

**CASE SHOWS LEVEL
OF SOPHISTICATION
IN DRUG TRADE**
By Amy Tunison

HANFORD – The arrest of Jose Pastor Magana, suspected to be one of the largest methamphetamine manufacturers and traffickers, in California, is an example, of how much more sophisticated the drug trade and the law enforcement that policies – has become.

"It's run just like a normal organization, it's like a business in structure," Cmdr. Mike Ortiz, a 16 year veteran of narcotics in law enforcement and head of the Kings County Narcotics Task Force, said.

"Magana was the president of the organization," he said.

The NTF was pivotal in the recent raid on the Hanford-based Magana organization. Working with state, federal, and local law enforcement, it has made over 20 arrests of prominent members of the business.

"Our game plan now is to attack organizations, not individuals," he said. "If, we can take the structure down, then the organization is erased."

Ortiz said there are two kinds of drug trafficking organizations, or DTO's family and non family based.

Magana's organization was family based, according to Ortiz, where family members such as brothers, uncles, sisters and cousins hold key positions of power in the upper echelons to maintain the organization.

"This tends to insulate it from law enforcement because if a member is arrested it is nearly impossible to get information from individuals because they aren't going to snitch on family," Ortiz said.

"Organizations like that can take hits, unless we can attack it as a whole," he said.

Ortiz said that in all his years in narcotics, Magana's organization was probably the most violent.

" I've dealt with several and this makes the top of my list as being violent," Ortiz said. "Our intelligence shows that many threats were made.

Head of meth ring a quiet neighbor

By Amy Tunison
Sentinel Staff Writer

HANFORD — Jose Pastor Magana, the suspected head of the largest methamphetamine distribution ring in California, along with his alleged subordinates were considered good neighbors.

Twenty-year-old Magana was taken into custody Wednesday from his home at the 11000 block of Evergreen Avenue in Hanford, a quiet middle-class neighborhood in Hanford where his neighbors had no problem with him.

"They've been here a short while, and always been decent and friendly enough," neighbor Jim Powers said.

"(The arrest) surprised me. I noticed there were always younger males over there but they never got out of line," he said.

In fact, Powers said that the biggest cause for concern was that Magana's pit bull puppies tended to get out of the yard, and he worried they'd be hit by a car.

A friend of Powers, Andy Perez, said that a residence near his home had also been the scene of an early morning raid at the same time.

"I just happened to get home for a few minutes and didn't know what was going on," Perez said. "I just seen different

Ralph Berrett/The Sentinel
PRESS CONFERENCE: Hanford Police Chief Brian DeCuir, flanked by California Highway Patrol division commander Danny Gilmore, left, and Kings County Sheriff Ken Marvin, right, discusses Wednesday's massive drug bust.

"To me they were good people," Perez said of Magana's underlings. "They seemed to be OK."

Magana's ring was under investigation for almost nine months before the early Wednesday morning sweep by 300 state, federal and local law enforcement agents.

Through surveillance, tips and informants, the agencies were able to build a case for probable cause, which led to the raid, according to law enforcement officials.

The agents served 32 war-

Back Page   The Sentinel -

Ralph Berrett/The Sentinel

RAIDED HOUSE: A house in South Hanford was residence to one of the suspects in the methamphetamine ring busted on Wednesday. Over 300 law officials representing federal, state and local jurisdictions took part in the massive arrest. A tally from the multiple drug sweeps netted a total of 15 pounds of meth valued at $7,000 a pound.

Bust

Continued from Page 1

rants and made 26 arrests, according to Kings County Sheriff Ken Marvin at a press conference Wednesday afternoon.

Marvin said the tally from the sweep by Wednesday afternoon totaled 15 pounds of meth worth $7,000 a pound wholesale, $45,000 when sold by the gram, "user" amounts of cocaine, and 141 marijuana plants were recovered at various residences around Kings and Tulare counties, as well as 30 handguns, rifles and other automatic weapons, $45,000 in cash and two vehicles.

Cmdr. Hal Chealander with the Kern County Sheriff's Department said that although a meth lab was not found Magana's organization was capable of producing 20-30 pounds of meth a week.

Chealander said these arrests would have a significant impact on the local meth trade, and that Magana's organization was a second-generation family business.

"It's a family organization," he said. "The father has been incarcerated for similar viola-tion. Magana picked it up from

The list of those arrested

BY SENTINEL STAFF

HANFORD — The following people were booked into the Kings County Jail in connection with the Jose Pastor Magana methamphetamine distribution ring. They are being held on state warrants.

Erik George Ortega, 20, of Hanford; Jose Ariel Flores, 19, of Hanford; Michael Wayne Shafer, 20, of Hanford; John Lujan Padilla, 20, of Hanford; Kevin Miles Cooper, 35, of Hanford; Jose Pacheco Torrez, 43, of Monson; Joseph Manuel Brieno, 22, of Hanford; Michael Lawson Fukano, 35, of Hanford; Ramon S. Mancilla, 20, of Hanford; Alejandro Reyes Flores, 24, of Hanford; Paul Fernandez Sandoval, 28, of Hanford; Alma Lorena I. Machado, 32, of Dinuba; Jerome

J. Landeros, 18, of Hanford; Rhonda Inman, 40, of Hanford; Brian Keith Dougherty, 31, of Hanford; Christopher Medrano, 20, of Hanford; Robert Paul Huerta, 19, of Hanford.

According to Kings County Deputy District Attorney Adam Nelson, all will be charged with at least one count of conspiracy to either manufacture or distribute meth, cocaine or marijuana, as well as possible charges of possession for sale or transport meth, cocaine or marijuana. Some will face gang enhancements, some will face weight of the narcotic enhancements. He said that all the defendants could be looking at a minimum of two years in jail if convicted.

Magana and eight others were booked in Fresno on federal warrants.

reached beyond family and into the community."

Carl Faller, assistant United States District Attorney in charge of the Fresno office, said

offer.

"We do what no one agency can do alone," Faller said. "Put a major distributor out of business."

THURSDAY, MAY 3, 2001
The Sentinel
Hanford, California

HEAD of METH RING
A QUIET NEIGHBOR
By Amy Tunison

HANFORD – Jose Pastor Magana, the suspected head of the largest methamphetamine Distribution ring in California, along with his alleged subordinates were considered good neighbors.

Twenty year old Magana was taken into custody Wednesday from his home at the 11000 block of Evergreen Avenue in Hanford, a quiet middle class neighborhood in Hanford where his neighbors had no problem with him.

"They've been here a short while, and always been decent and friendly enough," neighbor Jim Powers said.

"(The arrest) surprised me. I noticed there were always younger males over there but they never got out of line," he said.

In fact Powers said that the biggest cause for concern was that Magana's pit bull puppies tended to get out of the yard, and he worried they'd be hit by a car.

A friend of Powers, Andy Perez said that a residence near his home had also been the scene of an early morning raid at the same time.

"I just happened to get home for a few minutes and didn't know what was going on," Perez said. "I just seen different types, sheriffs, FBI, K9s."

"To me they were good people," Perez said of Magana's underlings. "They seemed to be OK."

Magana's ring was under investigation for almost nine months before the early Wednesday morning sweep by 300 state, federal and local law enforcement agents.

Through surveillance, tips and informants, the agencies were able to build a case for probable cause, which led to the raid, according to law enforcement officials.

The agents served 32 warrants and made 26 arrests, according to King County Sheriff Ken Marvin at press conference Wednesday afternoon.

Marvin said the tally from the sweep by Wednesday afternoon totaled 15 pounds of meth..........

Sandoval receives probation

Defendent in Magana drug ring gets a reduced sentence in return for testimony

By SENTINEL STAFF

HANFORD — The man who testified against two defendants charged with conspiring with the now-defunct Jose Pastor Magana drug ring was sentenced in court Monday morning.

Paul Fernandez Sandoval, 29, was sentenced to five years felony probation, 158 days in county jail (time he's already served) and fined $833 for his participation in the drug ring.

Chief Deputy District Attorney Patrick Hart said Sandoval's testimony was crucial.

"We (at the DA's Office) viewed (Sandoval's) testimony as being very important," Hart said.

Sandoval pleaded out on March 22 to charges of cultivation of marijuana and a gun enhancement.

His original charges included two counts of conspiracy to distribute narcotics, marijuana cultivation, committing a felony while on felony probation, being armed with a firearm, street gang enhancements and so on.

Deputy District Attorney Adam Nelson said Sandoval could have served 25 years to life in state prison if convicted of his original charges.

Magana's drug ring was subject to a nine-month investigation by the Kings County Narcotics Task Force, the FBI and other local, state and federal law enforcement agencies before a multi-agency sweep May 2 took most of Magana's alleged lieutenants and Magana himself into custody on conspiracy narcotics distribution charges.

Magana is awaiting trial in the federal court system.

**SANDOVAL
RECEIVES PROBATION**
Defendant in Magana drug
Ring gets a reduced sentence
In return for testimony

By Sentinel Staff

HANFORD – The man who testified against two defendants charged with conspiring with the now-defunct Jose Pastor Magana drug ring was sentenced in court Monday morning.

Paul Fernandez Sandoval, 29 was sentenced to five years felony probation, 158 days In county jail (time he's already served) and fined $833.00 for his participation in the drug ring.

Chief Deputy District Attorney Patrick Hart said Sandoval's testimony was crucial.

"We (at the DA's Office) viewed (Sandoval's) testimony as being very important." Hart said.

Sandoval pleaded out on March 22 to charges of cultivation of marijuana and a gun enhancement.

His original charges included two counts of conspiracy to distribute narcotics, marijuana cultivation, committing a felony while on felony probation, being armed with a firearm, street gang enhancements and so on.

Deputy District Attorney Adam Nelson said Sandoval could have served 25 years to life in state prison if convicted of his original charges.

Magana's drug ring was subject to a nine-month investigation by the Kings County Narcotics Task Force, the FBI and other local, state and federal law enforcement agencies before a multi-agency sweep May 2 took most of Magana's alleged lieutenants and Magana himself into custody on conspiracy narcotics distribution charges.

Magana is waiting trial in the federal court system.

Drug ring member Lobato sentenced to nine years in prison

By KARA MACHADO
Sentinel Reporter

HANFORD — The man found guilty of conspiracy drug charges that linked him to the now-defunct Jose Pastor Magana local drug organization was sentenced in a Kings County courtroom today.

Rudy Ben Lobato, 23, was sentenced to nine years in state prison this morning, according to Chief Deputy District Attorney Patrick Hart, for his conviction early last month of multiple counts of drug-related conspiracy charges. He could have faced more than 10 years.

Lobato was convicted March 8 of charges that included the sale, transportation, furnishing or giving away of the narcotic methamphetamine; possession of methamphetamine for the purpose of sales; the manufacturing of methamphetamine; and possession of marijuana for the purpose of sales. Lobato was also found guilty on an added methamphetamine weight enhancement.

At this morning's sentencing, Lobato's attorney Rudy Petilla implored that Judge Peter M. Schultz consider that Lobato is not a criminal but an addict, a stance that he held over from Lobato's trial.

Lobato was found to have been personally linked to Magana's drug ring, which was subject to a nine-month investigation by the Kings County Narcotics Task Force, the FBI and other local, state and federal law enforcement agencies. On May 2, 2001, a multi-agency sweep took most of Magana's alleged lieutenants and Magana himself into custody on conspiracy narcotics distribution charges. Magana is facing federal charges at this time.

Hart said the DA's Office was pleased with the outcome of Lobato's conviction.

"We obviously are happy with the results (of this trial)," Hart said. "(The Magana drug organization) was a major drug ring, (and taking it down) took a lot of narcotics off the street."

"I think (the May 2 sweep) made a major impact on the amount of street drugs available," Hart said. "And, of course, this drug ring was an exporter of drugs to other parts of the country, as well, so this bust has made a major impact in many ways."

Lobato, according to Hart, should be eligible for parole in approximately four and one-half years.

The reporter may be reached by e-mail at:
kmachado@sentinelnews.net

LOBATO SENTENCED
NINE YEARS IN PRISON

By Kara Machado
Sentinel Reporter

HANFORD – The man found guilty of conspiracy drug charges that linked him to the now defunct Jose Pastor Magana local drug organization was sentenced in a Kings County courtroom today.

Rudy Ben Lobato, 23, was sentenced to nine years in state prison this morning, according to Chief Deputy District Attorney Patrick Hart, for his conviction early last month of multiple counts of drug related conspiracy charges. He could have faced more than 10 years.

Lobato was convicted March 8 of charges that included the sale, transportation, furnishing or give away of the narcotic methamphetamine; possession of methamphetamine for the purpose of sales, the manufacturing of methamphetamine; and possession of marijuana for the purpose of sales. Lobato was also found guilty on an added methamphetamine weight enhancement.

At this morning's sentencing, Lobato's attorney Rudy Petilla implored that Judge Peter M. Shultz consider that Lobato is not a criminal but an addict, a stance that he held Over from Lobato's trial.

Lobato was found to have been personally linked to Magana's drug ring, which was subject to a nine-month investigation by the Kings County Narcotics Task Force, the FBI And other local law enforcement agencies. On May 2, 2001, a multi-agency sweep took most of Magana's alleged lieutenants and Magana himself into custody on conspiracy narcotics distribution charges at this time.

Hart said the DA's office was pleased with the outcome of Lobato's conviction.

"We obviously are happy with the results (of this trial)," Hart said, "(The Magana drug organization) was a major drug ring, (and taking it down) took a lot of narcotics off the street."

"I think (the May 2 sweep) made a major impact on the amount of street drugs available," Hart said. "And, of course, this drug ring was an exporter of drugs to other parts of the country, as well, so this bust has made a major impact in many ways."

Lobato, according to Hart, should be eligible for parole in approximately four and one half years.

www.newzcentral.com

THURSDAY

February 28, 2002

California — 50 cents

Star witness takes stand in drug trial

By KARA MACHADO
Sentinel Reporter

HANFORD — The trial concerning two defendants allegedly involved in a multi-agency drug sweep continued Wednesday, with one of the prosecution's star witnesses, Tony Araujo, taking the stand.

Araujo, a local businessman and Lakeside Union School District trustee, was questioned by Deputy District Attorney Adam Nelson on his involvement with the Jose Magana drug ring that allegedly included defendants Rudy Ben Lobato, 22, and Alejandro Reyes Flores, 24.

Nelson said that Lobato and Flores are being charged with conspiring to distribute the drugs methamphetamine and marijuana. Flores is additionally being charged with the possession of methamphetamine for sale, as well as an added gun enhancement.

Following FBI Special Agent Jonathan E. Crowe's testimony that Araujo helped to bring down the Magana drug ring by participating in undercover controlled drug buys and providing crucial information in that bust, Araujo took the stand

for the prosecution.

According to Araujo's testimony, his involvement with the Magana drug ring began when Lobato introduced him to Magana in the latter part of 1999. The relationship eventually evolved to where Magana was comfortable enough to share illegal information with Araujo.

Araujo said that he first met Lobato in 1999 when Lobato began to frequent Araujo's now-closed dairy and feed business for the purpose of purchasing Methyl Sulfonyl Methane. He said he later met Flores in late 1999/early 2000.

Araujo termed Lobato and Flores as one of the "less desirables" that began to swarm his store for MSM, an organic substance used as a cutting agent and for both ranching and human consumption purposes.

"MSM is an organic sulfur," Araujo testified. "It is used as a supplement for horses, it rejuvenates their joints; (it is) used for quicker repair of the joints."

"It's also a human supplement," Araujo said. "I personally take it and still do; (approximately) a fraction of a teaspoon

See TRIAL; Back Page

**STAR WITNESS TAKES
STAND IN DRUG TRIAL**

By Kara Machado
Sentinel Reporter

HANFORD – The trial concerning two defendants allegedly involved in a muti-agency drug sweep continued Wednesday, with one of the prosecution star witnesses, Tony Araujo, taking the stand.

Araujo, a local businessman and Lakeside Union School District trustee, was questioned by Deputy District Attorney Adam Nelson on his involvement with the Jose Magana drug ring that allegedly included defendants Rudy Ben Lobato, 22 and Alejandro Reyes Flores, 24.

Nelson said that Lobato and Flores are bring charged with conspiring to distribute the drugs methamphetamine and marijuana. Flores is additionally being charged with the possession of methamphetamine for sale, as well as an added gun enhancement.

Following FBI Special Agent Jonathan E. Crowe's testimony that Araujo helped to bring down the Magana drug ring by participating in undercover controlled drug buys and providing crucial information in that bust. Araujo took the stand for the prosecution.

According to Araujo's testimony, his involvement with the Magana drug ring began when Lobato introduced him to Magana in the latter part of 1999. The relationship eventually evolved to where Magana was comfortable enough to share illegal information with Araujo.

Araujo said that he first met Lobato in 1999 when Lobato began to frequent Araujo's now-closed dairy and feed business for the purpose of purchasing Methyl Sulfonyl Methane. He said he later met Flores in late 1999/early 2000.

Araujo termed Lobato and Flores as one of the "less desirables" that began to swarm his store for MSM, an organic substance used for cutting agent and for both ranching and human consumption purposes.

"MSM is an organic sulfur," Araujo testified. "It is used as a supplement for horses, it rejuvenates their joints; (it is) used for quicker repair of the joints."

"It's also a human supplement," Araujo said. "I personally take it and still do; (approximately) a fraction of a teaspoon with orange juice once daily."

Not long after Araujo first began to sell MSM in approximately early 1999, he said that an influx of younger customers began to request the product, making him somewhat suspicious. He then began to ask some of his customers why they were purchasing a high volume of MSM.

"I said (to Lobato), "you're sure going through a lot of MSM, and (Lobato) said, "I have arthritis in my knuckles," Araujo said. "And, he showed me his knuckles."

Araujo said his suspicions grew heavier when the FBI visited him in the summer of 2000 to question him about one of his customer's receipts for the sale of MSM. After cooperating fully with the FBI, Araujo said he continued to research into the alternative and illegal uses of MSM, research that he said eventually led to him re-contacting the FBI.

Trial

Continued from Page 1

with orange juice once daily."

Not long after Araujo first began to sell MSM in approximately early 1999, he said that an influx of younger customers began to request the product, making him somewhat suspicious. He then began to ask some of his customers why they were purchasing a high volume of MSM.

"I said (to Lobato), 'you're sure going through a lot of MSM,' and (Lobato) said, 'I have arthritis in my knuckles,'" Araujo said. "And, he showed me his knuckles."

Araujo said his suspicions grew heavier when the FBI visited him in the summer of 2000 to question him about one of his customer's receipts for the sale of MSM. After cooperating fully with the FBI, Araujo said he continued research into the alternative and illegal uses of MSM, research that he said

eventually led to him re-contacting the FBI.

Saying he had "a bad working relationship" with local law enforcement officials, prompting two lawsuits a few years back, Araujo said he decided not to go to local authorities and called the FBI officials whom he claimed to "get along well with."

Three FBI officials reportedly returned to Hanford from their field office in Fresno to listen to what Araujo had learned through his progressing relationship with Magana.

Araujo testified that he drove the FBI officials by the alleged "stash houses" in Hanford being rented by Magana for the alleged purpose of manufacturing and distributing narcotics. He said these locations were known to him through his MSM deliveries to Magana.

A couple of days later, Araujo said he received a call from FBI officials asking him to come to Fresno. He said he then agreed to go undercover to assist in bringing down

Magana's organization.

Defense attorneys claim that Araujo is not a credible witness, as he was motivated by the promise of immunity in his sales of MSM to members of the local drug culture, as well as an FBI payment of $35,000 for his help.

Araujo refutes these claims and said that he did not know he would be receiving a cash payment until after his work had already been completed, and a letter was signed that required his testimony in any upcoming trials.

Magana's ring was subject to a nine-month investigation by the Kings County Narcotics Task Force, the FBI and other local, state and federal agencies before a multi-agency sweep May 2 took most of Magana's alleged lieutenants and Magana himself into custody on conspiracy and narcotics distribution charges.

The reporter may be reached by e-mail at:

kmachado@sentinelnews.net

Saying he had "a bad working relationship" with local law enforcement officials, prompting two lawsuits a few years back, Araujo said he decided not to go to local authorities and called the FBI officials whom he claimed to "get along well with."

Three FBI officials reportedly returned to Hanford from their field office in Fresno to Listen to what Araujo had learned through his progressing relationship with Magana.

Araujo testified that he drove the FBI officials by the alleged 'stash houses" in Hanford being rented by Magana for the alleged purpose of manufacturing and distributing narcotics. He said these locations were known to him through his MSM deliveries to Magana.

A couple of days later, Araujo said he received a call from FBI officials asking him to come to Fresno. He said he then agreed to go undercover to assist in bringing down Magana's organization.

Defense attorneys claim that Araujo is not a credible witness, as he was motivated by the promise of immunity in his sales of MSM to members of the local drug culture, as well as an FBI payment of $35,000 for his help.

Araujo refutes these claims and said he did not know he would be receiving a cash payment until after his work had already been completed, and a letter was signed that required his testimony in any upcoming trials.

Magana's ring was subject to a nine-month investigation by the Kings County Narcotics Task Force, the FBI and other local, state and federal agencies before a multi-agency sweep May 2 took most of Magana's alleged lieutenants and Magana himself into custody on conspiracy and narcotics distribution charges.

U.S. Department of Justice
Federal Bureau of Investigation

is proud to recognize

Antonio Araujo

for your outstanding cooperation and assistance in connection with an investigation of great importance. The FBI's ability to carry out its investigative responsibilities to the American people has been greatly enhanced through your help, and you can be very proud of your valuable contributions to the success achieved.

July 2001
Date

Thomas J. Pickard
Acting Director
Federal Bureau of Investigation